D0427091

APPEARANCE AND REALITY IN INTERNATIONAL RELATIONS

APPEARANCE AND REALITY IN INTERNATIONAL RELATIONS

GRANT HUGO

1970
COLUMBIA UNIVERSITY PRESS
NEW YORK

Published 1970 in Great Britain by
Chatto & Windus Ltd., London, and in Canada
by Clarke, Irwin & Co. Ltd., Toronto

Copyright © Grant Hugo 1970
ISBN: 0 231 03468 7
Library of Congress Catalog Card Number: 72-137420
Printed in Great Britain

I have called it Appearance and Reality. . . .
There is no excuse for my making use of
the title of so celebrated a book except that
it so admirably suits my story.

SOMERSET MAUGHAM

W. S. Maugham, *Complete Short Stories*, Volume I

CONTENTS

INTRODUCTION

'Why do the nations so furiously rage together,
and why do the people imagine a vain thing?'[1]

THIS book attempts to analyse some of the ideas
commonly employed by governments in the conduct of international relations. Unlike the author's
previous work – *Britain in Tomorrow's World: Principles
of Foreign Policy*[2] – it does not offer a complete and self-
contained thesis. The hundred-odd nation states of the
modern world are too various and the possible combinations and permutations of their diverse interests and
aspirations are too numerous to be reduced to a single
system or to be considered within the compass of a single
book. What can be attempted for one country can
scarcely even be conceived for so many.

Instead this is a set of variations on a single theme, an
endeavour to illustrate by examples drawn from many
countries and from various periods of recent history,
the proposition that the quarrels of mankind are aggravated by misunderstanding and that their consequences
might perhaps be mitigated if governments were to
precede their decisions by a more methodical process of
analysis.

[1] Jennens and Handel, 'Messiah'.
[2] Chatto & Windus 1969.

9

In itself this is not a particularly original notion. From the earliest days of civilization men have endeavoured to extract general principles from particular experiences and to embody the lessons of the past in precepts for the future. The excuse for another attempt is equally elementary: the nations still rage furiously together and the successes of the scientists have greatly increased the perils of imagining a vain thing, a tendency from which no philosopher has yet been able to deliver the peoples of the world and their rulers.

Perhaps some of these philosophers failed because they attempted too much. They sought comprehensive systems of universal validity. They, or their successors, then blamed the failure of these systems on the weakness, vice, folly and incapacity of the world's statesmen. Many, of whom Plato was hardly the first, nor Lord Russell the last, then concluded that only the imposition of a single despotism could save mankind from its own dissensions.

No such ambitious proposal is here advanced. This book accepts the ills of the world and offers no cure for them, only a minor palliative for a particular class of affliction: the international dispute that is needlessly aggravated because the participants are more concerned with motives than with consequences. When governments have to choose between different courses of action, they are accustomed to argue either that a particular decision was intrinsically meritorious or else that it was forced upon them by the objectionable act of another government. It will here be contended that such arguments are often untrue, usually misleading and always irrelevant. The significance of an action depends more on its concrete results than on its antecedents or on the merits of the motives that prompted it.

The central argument of this book is thus that some methods of reaching decisions are better than others, because decisions thus arrived at are rather more likely to have advantageous results. The approach preferred is described as realistic on the assumption that a concrete result is more real than a motive, whether this motive is emotional, ethical or ideological. Metaphysically, of course, this is a most questionable assumption, but it is one which derives a certain rough and ready support from the observable facts of twentieth-century international existence. Anyone who has smelt a battlefield, clambered among the ruins of a bombed city, visited a refugee camp, is likely to have been more impressed by the tangible results of human decisions than by the motives which prompted them. And these were puny results by comparison with those to be expected from future decisions. Technology, which might be defined as a process of increasing the disproportion between cause and effect, has incalculably multiplied the potential consequences of human decisions, but has not significantly extended the motives by which men and governments are actuated. Whether or not a particular motive, or an inter-action of motives, was ever more important than one death, or a thousand deaths, or the thirty million deaths of the Second World War, the mere attrition of arithmetic has now diminished that importance and, as the bill of mortality approaches the sum of the species, must eventually extinguish it altogether.

Many people, however, while admitting that the results of what they would call bad motives can today be worse than ever before, would deny that good motives could have equally ill effects. This is not a contention accepted in the present work, which insists that the only Real difference between one decision and another is to be discerned in the concrete results of those decisions, any distinction between the originating motives being only Apparent and, in practice, as misleading as it is usually irrelevant.

As this is naturally a somewhat controversial view, the first chapter is accordingly devoted to an analysis of some of the discrepancies between the Apparent motives of historical decisions and the Real results. Thus prepared the reader may find it easier to approach the central core of the book – the section devoted to Appearance and Reality. This criticizes, in the light of selected examples, some of the more prevalent methods of approaching international problems and endeavours to suggest practical alternatives. The remainder of the book is devoted to an examination, again in the light of specific instances, of some of the theoretical consequences of the central argument together with certain possible exceptions or extensions. The purpose is to consider the usefulness, to those who have to take decisions, of abstract principles or concepts.

Because these theoretical arguments are intended to be of practical utility they have, wherever possible, been illustrated by the analysis of problems that have already arisen. This has involved frequent critical reference to the actual conduct of various governments, but all such criticism, whether favourable or otherwise, is directed solely to the methods employed in reaching decisions and all judgements are based on the results achieved.

12

INTRODUCTION

The prejudices of the author may be apparent but will, it is hoped, prove irrelevant. His object has been to offer a small contribution to the methodological theory of international relations and not to advocate any particular interest, ideology or policy.

Nevertheless, if this book − or any other on the same subject − is to be useful, it must not lose sight of its only effective readership: the people who might one day be able to influence decisions. That is why the assumption has been made that decisions in international disputes are taken by reasonable men, whose choices can be influenced by the argument that some methods are more likely than others to have advantageous results. This is a view nowadays much disputed and the curious reader may wish to consult a compendium of which the title alone bears any resemblance to the present work: *Image and Reality in World Politics*.[1] There he will find argued the propositions that the international system is 'pathological'; that its manipulators, though not actually insane, are liable to 'certain occupational diseases' which impair their perception of reality and their ability to reach rational decisions;[2] that 'there is little likelihood that even genuine attempts to resolve the issues will have the desired effect'[3] and that 'multivariant analysis' has 'revealed hostility to be the best predictor of action'.[4]

These are interesting and important ideas. So is Dr. L'Etang's analysis of the extent to which disease and its

[1] Edited by John C. Farrell and Asa P. Smith (Columbia University Press 1968).

[2] Kenneth E. Boulding, 'The Learning and Reality-Testing Process in the International System'.

[3] Ole R. Holsti, 'Cognitive Dynamics and Images of the Enemy'.

[4] Robert C. North, 'Perception and Action in the 1914 Crisis'.

treatment may distort the judgement of statesmen.[5] So are all the various theories which depict individual leaders as the puppets of vast impersonal forces. It is right that the limitations on human initiative should be exhaustively explored and discussed. But the doctrines of behaviourism and determinism do not find their appropriate place in a book which aspires, however humbly, to practical utility. If politicians and diplomats are as Pavlov's dogs, they are beyond the reach of any-one's arguments; if bodily ailments have impaired their mental faculties, doctors are more necessary than writers; if vast, impersonal forces are responsible, it is unlikely that these can read. There is not much point in trying to influence decisions unless someone is supposed to be capable of taking them.

There is a further consideration. Presumptuous and superficial though it may seem to disregard the varied evidence of determinism, most of its advocates admit the existence of certain exceptions. Professors, for instance, are notoriously immune from the afflictions of politicians and even the latter may have their rational moments, their intervals of free-will. If one of these happened to coincide with a fleeting recollection of something once read, the smallest grain of theory might just tip a trembling balance. The odds against it are enormous, but, until the world is much altered, rather better than the chances of the behaviourists of putting matters right with electro-convulsion or aversion therapy. The philosopher's best hope of progress still depends on the persuasion of Princes, which demands a decent

[5] Hugh L'Etang, *The Pathology of Leadership* (Heinemann Medical Books 1969).

pretence that they too have minds to make up. Academic advice based on other assumptions is apt to fall on ears that are wilfully deaf.

One final observation may be of interest. The central argument of the book is that actions should be decided in the light of their likely consequences, a precept that is practical only if these consequences can be predicted with some degree of accuracy. Chapter 3 not only examines this problem in general terms, but also puts forward a specific prediction. To enable the reader to appreciate the value of this prediction and, consequently, of the theoretical arguments on which it is based, he should know that this chapter was written before the rest of the book, having originally been intended as a separate article, and is now reproduced exactly as it was originally rejected by an impercipient editor in October 1968. By the time this book eventually emerges from the leisurely processes of publication, therefore, events should have provided a practical test of one aspect of its theories.

I

CANT IN FOREIGN POLICY

'My dear friend, clear your mind of cant . . . you may talk in this manner; it is a mode of talking in society; but don't think foolishly.'

Johnson[1]

CANT has so long and so variously diversified the texture of international relations that any brief examination must necessarily concentrate on a single aspect of this complex and controversial phenomenon. We shall not, for instance, here be concerned with cant as an esoteric language intended to confuse the vulgar while conveying a specific meaning to initiates, an important function in the nineteenth century, when an 'unfriendly act' was a phrase more precisely and convincingly minatory than such later formulations as 'we are filled with determination to use force to crush the aggressors'.[2] The progressive inflation of diplomatic language and its increasing divorce from consequential action have nowadays destroyed this once useful application of cant.

Nor is it necessary to consider, intriguing though such a study might be, the stylistic mannerisms of particular governments. The British, for instance, delight in

---

[1] Boswell, *Life of Johnson*.
[2] Marshal Bulganin to Sir A. Eden, 5 November 1956, quoted in Anthony Eden, *Full Circle*, Chapter 8 (Cassell 1960).

such phrases as 'British public opinion attaches great importance to the due execution of the Article in question . . .',[1] whereas the Russians, in a manner reminiscent of Macaulay's 'every schoolboy knows who imprisoned Montezuma and who strangled Atahualpa',[2] prefer 'in no other way is it possible to explain the unalterable fact'.[3] The demonstrable untruth of such assertions — one could spend an entire day interrogating pedestrians in Piccadilly without discovering a single British subject who had even heard of Article 14(d) of the Agreement on the Cessation of Hostilities in Vietnam — is not deliberate, or systematic or consequential: it is the merest literary aberration, an uncontrolled impetuosity of expression.

Deliberate deception, however, is not a necessary or even a distinguishing characteristic of cant. Those addicted to this mode of expression or cast of thought may believe their own words; they may be using conventionally acceptable language to clothe controversial ideas; or they may be trying to disguise their meaning. What counts is not the sincerity of the speaker but the relationship between the impression naturally created by his words and their obvious practical implications. In the language of cant there is usually a marked discrepancy between the satisfaction, approval, toleration or indifference to be expected from those who accept the words used at their face value and the sentiments aroused in those who believe they have comprehended the full intentions, implications or assumptions of an apparently

[1] Command 2834, *Documents relating to British Involvement in the Indo-China Conflict*, doc. 45 (H.M.S.O.).

[2] Thomas Babington Macaulay, *Historical Essays*.

[3] Command 2834, doc. 84.

innocuous phraseology. It is the extent of this discrepancy, rather than the degree of correspondence with
objective truth, that distinguishes cant from tact. When
a diplomatist declines an invitation because of a prior
engagement, he may be telling a flat lie, but he is giving
tactful expression to a concrete and unambiguous intention: not to accept. When the United States Strategic
Air Command proclaim 'peace is our profession', they
are indulging in cant, even if elaborate and sophisticated
arguments might be adduced to support their assertion.
The discrepancy between the natural meaning of 'peace'
and the real prospect of thermo-nuclear megadeaths is
excessive.

Cant, therefore, will be considered here as a mode of
expression, or a cast of thought, of which the effect —
irrespective of the motive — is to create a misleading
discrepancy between the natural meaning of words and
their practical significance, a discrepancy even more
dangerous when, as often happens, the speaker is as
much misled as his audience.

This is a subjective and question-begging definition,
but cant resembles sin: it is deplorable; it is widespread
and it is committed exclusively by other people. It
would thus be misleading — indeed, it might even be
regarded as cant — to claim a high degree of objectivity
or general acceptance for the attempt that follows to
isolate from actual examples the specific characteristics
of this phenomenon. Any description or definition
necessarily implies certain prior assumptions of a political or quasi-philosophical character. Any conclusions
reached may thus prove repugnant to those who reject
their premises. These are those of realism and relativity:

that, in the world as it exists, the language of governments has to be assessed by the degree of its approximation to their actions and that these actions have to be judged by their results.

This is an approach which extends the customary frontiers of cant beyond the utterances of foreign governments or even of those native statesmen of whom the reader happens to disapprove. Indeed, it is fundamental to the present argument that cant is a universal phenomenon confined to no one nation, class of men or set of ideas. It is to be found on both sides of most disputes and there have been many diplomatic exchanges, even between nation-states of similar traditions and social structures, in which each could sincerely contrast their own candour with the other's cant.

A classical example is the report by the British Ambassador in Berlin of his final interview with the German Chancellor on 4 August 1914:

'I found the Chancellor very agitated. His Excellency at once began a harangue, which lasted for about twenty minutes. He said that the step taken by His Majesty's Government was terrible to a degree; just for a word – "neutrality", a word which in war had so often been disregarded – just for a scrap of paper Great Britain was going to make war on a kindred nation who desired nothing better than to be friends with her. All his efforts in that direction had been rendered useless by this last terrible step, and the policy to which, as I knew, he had devoted himself since his accession to office had tumbled down like a house of cards. What we had done was unthinkable; it was like striking a man from behind while he was fighting for his life against two assailants. He held Great Britain responsible for all the terrible events that might happen. I protested strongly against that statement, and said that, in the same way as he and Herr von Jagow wished me to understand that for strategical reasons it was a matter of life and death to Germany to advance through Belgium and violate the latter's neutrality, so I would wish him to understand that it was, so to speak, a matter of "life and death" for the honour of Great Britain that she should keep her solemn engagement to do her utmost to defend Belgium's neutrality if attacked. That solemn compact simply had to be kept, or what confidence could anyone have in engagements given by Great Britain in the future? The Chancellor said, "But at what price will that compact have been kept. Has the British Government thought of that?"[1]

There is no reason to doubt Bethman-Hollweg's sincerity (Harold Nicolson, who knew him personally, described him as sharing with Sir Edward Grey 'the honour of being, alone of pre-war statesmen, morally unassailable')[2] but few British readers have failed to detect the discrepancy between his professions of friendship and the underlying assumptions and implications so obviously revealed by the policy of his government. Yet, when one ponders on Bethman-Hollweg's final question, when one recalls Hardinge's famous minute on the British guarantee to Belgium,[3] when one studies

[1] Sir E. Goschen to Sir E. Grey, quoted in Guy Chapman, *Vain Glory* (Cassell 1937).

[2] Harold Nicolson, *Lord Carnock* (Constable 1930).

[3] Gooch & Temperley, *British Documents on the Origins of the War,* Vol. VIII (H.M.S.O.). Mr. Eyre Crowe of the Foreign Office had written a memorandum on 15 November 1908 concerning British obligations towards Belgium, which concluded:

'Great Britain is liable for the maintenance of Belgian neutrality whenever either Belgium or any of the guaranteeing Powers are in need of, and demand, assistance in opposing its violation.'

On which Sir Charles Hardinge, then Permanent Under-Secretary, minuted:

'The liability undoubtedly exists as stated above, but whether we

the various interpretations accorded by British governments – before or after 1914 – to the 'honour of Great
Britain', can one acquit Sir E. Goschen of an equal
indulgence in cant?

Each of the participants in this dramatic dialogue was
surely employing language that was only metaphorically
related to the practical problems at issue. The neutrality
of Belgium had not yet been threatened when the French
Ambassador in London, relying on the secret staff talks
concealed by Sir Edward Grey from Parliament (and
for long even from his colleagues) exclaimed on 1 August:
'j'attends de savoir si le mot honneur doit être rayé du
vocabulaire anglais.'[1] Nor was it his opinion alone that
the honour of England was at stake before Belgium was
invaded: the Permanent Under-Secretary of the Foreign
Office (by this time the less cynical Sir Arthur Nicolson)
had already protested to Sir Edward Grey: 'you will
render us a by-word among nations'.[1] As for Bethman-
Hollweg, he had been warned on 29 July that, if France
were attacked, Britain would not long stand aside and
had taken the warning seriously enough to send a frantic,
if futile, telegram to Vienna that Germany 'must decline
to be irresponsibly dragged into a world war'.[1]

[1] Nicolson, op. cit.

could be called upon to carry out our obligation and to vindicate the
neutrality of Belgium in opposing its violation must necessarily depend
on our policy at the time and the circumstances of the moment. Supposing
that France violated the neutrality of Belgium in a war against Germany,
it is, under present circumstances, doubtful whether England or Russia
would move a finger to maintain Belgian neutrality, which [sic] if the
neutrality of Belgium were violated by Germany it is probable that the
converse would be the case.'

This observation the 'morally unassailable' Sir Edward Grey found
'to the point'.

It would, of course, be unreasonable to suggest that, on the 4th of August 1914, there still existed a serious possibility of arresting the fatal avalanche of events. Goschen and Bethman-Hollweg were performing a Wagnerian duet, a cadenza to a civilization that had already entered its irreversible agony. Nevertheless each was faithfully representing the illusions of his government and their exchange constitutes a revealing example of cant in its most high-minded, most plausible and most pernicious form. Neither was lying: each was selecting certain aspects of the situation and emphasizing these at the expense of others omitted. Both preferred metaphors and abstractions to any analysis of concrete cause and effect: naval dispositions, the Schlieffen Plan, the movements of mobilizing armies. Only Bethman-Hollweg's final question hints at any awareness of the real issues at stake, issues undreamt of in London, where the Foreign Secretary had already told an ignorant House of Commons that:

'if we are engaged in war, we shall suffer but little more than we shall suffer if we stand aside.'[1]

It is, perhaps, in its sublimation of human suffering, in its abstraction of the argument from the details of death and destruction, from the tedious particulars of profit and loss, that the most characteristic feature of cant is to be detected. When a situation is described or a course of action explained or a result predicted, not in concrete, material and ultimately verifiable terms, but

[1] A. J. P. Taylor has explained that 'by suffering he meant only the interruption of British trade with the continent of Europe'. Taylor, *The Struggle for Mastery in Europe* (Oxford University Press 1954).

by the use of abstractions or metaphors calculated to evoke a particular emotional response, there is usually cause to suspect the presence of cant.

Compare, for instance, these two statements:

'Our strategic policy must continue to be the deterrence of a deliberate nuclear attack against the United States or its allies . . . what level of potential destruction would have to be achieved to maintain that deterrence? . . . In the case of the Soviet Union, I would judge that a capability on our part to destroy, say, one-fifth to one-fourth of her population and one-half of her industrial capacity would serve as an effective deterrent.'[1]

'In recent months attacks on South Vietnam were stepped up. Thus it became necessary to increase our response and make attacks by air. This is not a change of purpose. It is a change in what we believe that purpose required. We do this in order to slow down aggression.

We do this to increase the confidence of the brave people of South Vietnam who have bravely borne this brutal battle for so many years and with so many casualties.

And we do this to convince the leaders of North Vietnam – and all who seek to share their conquest – of a simple fact:

We will not be defeated. We will not grow tired. We will not withdraw, either openly or under the cloak of a meaningless agreement.

We know that air attacks alone will not accomplish all these purposes. But it is our best and prayerful judgement that they are a necessary part of the surest road to peace.'[2]

Both these predictions regarding the deterrent effects of aerial bombardment are representative extracts from much longer public statements, each of which is throughout its length stylistically consistent with the portion

[1] Statement to Congress as reproduced in Robert S. McNamara, *The Essence of Security* (Hodder & Stoughton 1968).

[2] Speech by President Johnson on 7 April 1965 as reproduced in Command 2756 of 1965, doc. 21 (H.M.S.O.).

quoted. The first is always concrete, dispassionate and factual: the objective is assumed, not argued, and the means of its attainment are described with cold precision. The second is a prolonged appeal for emotional approval, in which the objective is described in abstract and meta-phorical terms, but nothing whatever is said concerning the nature of the 'air attacks' or their expected results. Even an opponent of Mr. McNamara's policies could scarcely accuse him of cant in their expression, but it would be difficult for anyone to acquit President Johnson of the same charge, particularly in his choice of the epithet 'prayerful' in justifying his decision to bomb North Vietnam.

It may be objected that rhetorical utterance is a necessary element in political leadership and that public speeches on urgent and important topics can not be expected to meet the fastidious criteria of the man of letters or to survive the retrospective judgement of the historian. But the mode of expression always reveals the cast of thought and it is probably more than a coincidence that, even without the assistance of prayer, Mr. McNamara's judgement has so far proved more accurate than President Johnson's. Someone who predicts that specific actions will have concrete results is more likely to be right than someone who talks, and thinks, in terms of 'the surest road to peace'.

Unfortunately it is easier to multiply instances of the use of cant than to arrive at a precise and generally acceptable definition of its characteristics. It may be true that cant usually entails an abstract and metaphorical appeal to emotion, but not all such exhortations are necessarily to be classed as cant. Consider, for instance, the following passage of rhetoric:

> 'Now that I have taken up my office as Prime Minister and Minister of Defence I look back to our meetings in Rome and feel a desire to speak words of goodwill to you as Chief of the Italian nation across what seems to be a swiftly-widening gulf. Is it too late to stop a river of blood from flowing between the British and Italian peoples? We can no doubt inflict grievous injuries upon one another and maul each other cruelly and darken the Mediterranean with our strife. If you so decree, it must be so; but I declare that I have never been the enemy of Italian greatness, nor ever at heart the foe of the Italian law-giver. It is idle to predict the course of the great battles now raging in Europe, but I am sure that whatever may happen on the Continent England will go on to the end, even quite alone, as we have done before, and I believe with some assurance that we shall be aided in increasing measure by the United States and, indeed, by all the Americas.'[1]

Here indeed is hyperbole and a luxuriance of emotive abstraction. Yet analysis of this florid language reveals its close concern with the practical situation – the danger of war with Italy; an objective assessment of its mutual disadvantages; a realistic admission that the outcome of the campaign in France was uncertain and an equally realistic forecast that Britain would continue the fight in the confident expectation of American assistance. Above all, there is an entire absence of any one-sided appeal to moral principles. Even the denial of personal enmity – perhaps the nearest approach to cant – is historically tenable and, in the Head of a new Government, relevant. Otherwise the arguments adduced for the avoidance of war rely entirely on considerations of common interest

[1] Winston Churchill, *Their Finest Hour* (Cassell 1944).

and, with some alteration of language, could equally well have been drafted for Mussolini by his own officials.

Conversely, when the sober Mr. McNamara turns his attention to Vietnam, he abandons his usual endeavour dispassionately to assess and, wherever possible, to quantify the capacities and intention of his opponents, for a one-sided appeal to abstraction:

> 'we find ourselves engaged in a conflict with North Vietnam and its South Vietnamese supporters to preserve the principle that political change must not be brought about by externally directed violence and military force.'[1]

The language may be cool, but the cant is unmistakable. Even if the principle were valid, even if it had been consistently observed by the United States, even if the adverb 'externally' could properly be applied to North Vietnam, that conflict has seen no monopoly of 'externally directed violence and military force'. Larger questions have seldom been more concisely begged.

Indeed, although the applications of cant are infinite and its characteristics various, it may perhaps be most easily identified by the preference shown by its practitioners for explaining their actions in terms of their own motives and principles. It is a common observation of everyday life that actions of benevolence seldom require or receive any moral justification. The man who explains his motives and invokes his principles does so to excuse himself for disobliging you. In international exchanges it is in their disputes that governments endeavour:

> 'to make up what was wanting in the justice of their cause . . . by a cant and sophistical way of expression.'[2]

[1] McNamara, op. cit.
[2] Carte, *History of England*, quoted in the *Oxford English Dictionary* as an early example.

The full implications of this practice are often missed by those who seize only on the plentiful evidence of inconsistency in the proclamation of principles. On 24 August 1939, for instance, the British Prime Minister told an acquiescent House of Commons that:

> 'We want to see established an international order based upon mutual understanding and mutual confidence, and we cannot build such an order unless it conforms to certain principles which are essential to the establishment of confidence and trust. Those principles must include the observance of international undertakings when they have once been entered into . . . if despite our efforts to find the way of peace . . .[1] we find ourselves forced to embark upon a struggle which is bound to be fraught with suffering and misery for all mankind and the end of which no man can foresee, if that should happen, we shall be fighting for the preservation of those principles of which I have spoken, the destruction of which would involve the destruction of all possibility of peace and security for the peoples of the world.'[2]

This Prime Minister was Neville Chamberlain, who, as Chancellor of the Exchequer, had earlier reminded the House that:

> 'When we are told that contracts must be kept sacred, and that we must on no account depart from the obligations we have undertaken, it must not be forgotten that we have other obligations and responsibilities, obligations not only to our own countrymen but to many millions of human beings throughout the world, whose happiness or misery may depend upon how far the fulfillment of these obligations is insisted upon on the one side and met on the other.'[3]

[1] It is curious how similar phrases recur on the lips of belligerence – compare the earlier quotation from President Johnson – 'the surest road to peace'.

[2] *The Penguin Hansard* (Penguin Books 1940).

[3] *Hansard*, 14 December 1932, Vol. 273, col. 354.

If any of the thirty million human beings who perished in that struggle were ever aware of the principles on which they died, some of them might have preferred Chamberlain's earlier pronouncement to his second thoughts, but, if they had realized that this heart-warming elevation of human happiness over the sanctity of contracts was no more than an excuse for ceasing repayment of an American loan, they might have been excused the cynical view that the element of cant was equally redolent in each, as it was in all the other declarations of principle made by every one of the leaders of the warring nations. If the examples quoted in these pages have been selected primarily from English-speaking sources, it is not for any lack of corresponding utterances in other languages. Cant is international, but English-speaking readers need less convincing of its existence among foreigners.

But inconsistency, though a frequent characteristic, is no more a necessary attribute of cant than untruth, insincerity or rhetorical and inappropriate language. It is the invocation of principles and the attribution of motives that identifies cant and not the merits of either. The statesman who sincerely believes himself to be defending righteous action in a good cause is still guilty of cant if he is more concerned with his own virtue than with the predictable and concrete results of his action. In the thermo-nuclear age the old saying that the road to Hell is paved with good intentions has acquired a new and more frightening significance. As long as Russian and American rulers are actuated by calculation, we may hope to survive in the knowledge that:

'it is now impossible for either the United States or the Soviet Union to achieve a meaningful victory over the other in a strategic nuclear exchange.'[1]

But, if principles are allowed to predominate over considerations of profit and loss, then the prospects for the human race are sombre indeed. Interest is a universal language and, properly comprehended, can lead men to compromise: principles divide them and, if pressed to their different conclusions, can only tend, through bewilderment and exasperation, to final disaster.[2]

The principles thus condemned are naturally those, whether ethical, ideological or religious, solely concerned with the intrinsic nature and quality of actions without regard to their likely results. There is no necessarily pernicious element in those principles of political conduct intended only to assist statesmen in the making of advantageous choices or in predicting the consequences of their decisions. Theory has its proper place in politics as long as it is rooted in the real world and firmly directed towards practical objectives. It is the principles which justify means, not by their rationally expected results, but by the motives of those who select them, that are to be avoided.

It is because cant is the language of such principles that it is dangerous – and would still be dangerous even if the principles professed were intrinsically valid and consistently applied. These principles and their cant are the expression of irresponsibility: the negation of that ancient maxim of English law that reasonable men may be presumed to intend the natural consequences of their

[1] McNamara, op. cit.
[2] For a fuller exposition of this thesis see Grant Hugo, op. cit.

acts. Once motives are allowed to excuse results, foreign policy is divorced from the rule of reason and leads inevitably, but on an immeasurably larger and more disastrous scale, to the crime passionnel. If Scottish readers will forgive the solecism of preferring the rhythm to the original sense, it is worth recalling that one of the earliest instances of the word in the *Oxford English Dictionary* is the profoundly symbolic phrase: 'cant men and cruel.' From the malign influence of such men may reason, cynicism and the dispassionate analysis of the probable deliver us all.

2

APPEARANCE AND REALITY

'I permit myself a trite remark. It is strange that men, inhabitants for so short a while of an alien and inhuman world, should go out of their way to cause themselves so much unhappiness.'

Somerset Maugham[1]

HAVING already considered some of the consequences of good intentions, it is time to examine other approaches to the human dilemma, always remembering that, in international affairs, the choice of remedies and even the resolution to apply them may often prove a lesser source of difficulty than the identification of the problem. In the hope of assisting this process the present chapter will accordingly concentrate on seeking a distinction between the Real and the Apparent nature of international problems. Such a distinction is not intended for philosophers, nor would it satisfy their more exacting standards, but for those required to take practical decisions.

The starting-point is the obvious proposition that understanding a problem is the necessary first step towards its solution. Unfortunately the normal method of attaining understanding — careful study of full and accurate information — is seldom available to those who

[1] W. S. Maugham, 'The Creative Impulse', *Complete Short Stories*, Vol. II (Heinemann).

have to take decisions in the field of international affairs. Even many years afterwards historians often find it difficult to agree on the facts of a particular situation: who did what, the meaning of their words and, above all, the intentions behind their actions. At the moment of choice the Foreign Minister concerned has less information than the historian and no time to sift the true from the false. The longer he reflects on the nature of the problem before him, the greater the likelihood that fresh events will transform it. Every kind of pressure impels him to urgent decision and hence to snap judgement. He must seize on the essence of the situation and, from the cloud of uncertain circumstances, isolate the questions to be answered at once. Moreover, where the historian concentrates his efforts, perhaps for years, on the solution of a single puzzle, the Foreign Minister must dissipate his attention among a host of unrelated issues, identifying, defining and solving his problems without interrupting the transaction of current business.

Only the most drastic simplification makes his task possible at all. He is not the hospital physician who can demand a dozen clinical tests before considering a diagnosis, but the harassed slum doctor whose right hand fumbles for his prescription pad before the left has quitted the patient's pulse. It follows that his judgement depends primarily on his preconceptions: he necessarily has prior notions of what constitutes a problem, what determines its importance, what kind of features are likely to provide its essence. Such preconceptions can be very different and, when they are, will result in differing analyses of the same problem and hence in the adoption of different measures for its solution.

When these problems are examined with the retrospective calm and deliberation of the historian, it often appears that the eventual outcome bore little relation to the original intentions of those concerned. Sometimes this may be ascribed to a wrong choice of method, occasionally to an attempt at the impossible. But often, so at least it seems to the detached observer, there was such a discrepancy between initial decisions and eventual results as to suggest a fundamental misconception of the original problem. The doctor's error did not lie in his choice of medicines, but in his failure to perceive that the swollen ankle indicated not gout, but a fracture.

Foreign affairs, unfortunately, can not aspire to even the limited and provisional certainties of medicine. There is no philosophical sense, no metaphysical validity, in the claim that one aspect, one presentation of a particular problem is nearer to ultimate truth than another. The more people are concerned with a particular problem the more Appearances it will present, each derived from a different set of preconceptions. The most that could ever be claimed for any conception of the Reality of international problems would be that this would be accepted as a half-truth by most of the participants and that, if made the basis for decisions, these might prove correct more often than not. The test of Reality, therefore, is its ability to command at least partial acceptance from the proponents of otherwise incompatible ideas; its justification is its ability to describe problems in terms that usefully suggest a probable solution.

What we are seeking is a way of looking at international problems that might help harassed practitioners to decide quickly and simply what kind of question they ought to ask. If the distinction between Appearance and Reality is useful, it follows that some of the obvious questions are misleading and irrelevant, so that any answers they evoke are likely to produce unsatisfactory results. It does not follow, however, that even an appropriately stated question will always elicit a correct answer leading to desirable consequences. But an approximate answer to the right question may stand a better chance than a good answer to the wrong one. Our search, therefore, is not for ultimate truth, but for a rule of thumb, a rough and ready guide to distinguishing the features that constitute the essence of international problems.

I — PROBLEMS AS DISPUTES

The first step is to define the nature of the problems to be considered: disputes among nation-states.

These do not, perhaps, constitute the only international problems. Indeed, it might be argued that a preoccupation with disputes was one of the misconceptions earlier mentioned. It would be hard to convince a Martian that the precise type of misgovernment to afflict South Vietnam or the variety of the Semitic race that ought to inhabit the small area once known as Palestine could be regarded as problems at all equivalent in importance to the human race to the fundamental and universal dilemmas of over-population and inadequate resources. Even terrestrial commentators (though these do not include many Arabs, Israelis or Vietnamese) have insisted that the world's statesmen should now be concentrating their attention on reducing the birth-rate, increasing the production of food and conserving, or else synthesizing, the fossil fuels.

That these and other problems inseparable from the survival of the species ought to receive attention is undeniable. In a more rationally organized world every government would include a Minister of Human Cooperation with the task of promoting generally acceptable solutions. Meanwhile it is a fact and, from certain points of view, not altogether irrational, that one of the principal branches of every government is the Ministry of Human Strife, commonly known as the Ministry of Foreign Affairs. It may or may not be true — although the predictions of Malthus offer a dubious precedent — that the year 2500 will see an overcrowded planet in the grip of famine and devoid of the fuels and raw materials essential to the maintenance of a tolerable existence. But it is also true that the governments of the Soviet Union and the United States already possess the power to eliminate most of the human race, not in A.D. 2500, but tomorrow. It is not unreasonable to regard this threat as more imminent, more probable and consequently more important than remoter perils. Similarly, if under some apparently trivial dispute between less formidable governments there lies the hidden danger of an early confrontation of the Super-Powers, the dispute inevitably acquires an importance unrelated to the motives or the capacities of the contestants themselves. Governments can not be blamed for according priority to those problems which, if neither solved nor alleviated, might render nugatory the consideration of any others.

There is also, if we remove ourselves from the scale of eternity to that of everyday life, a more human factor. The rulers of the world are mostly elderly men and, occasionally, women. Few of them have much reason to expect more than ten years of power or even twenty of active existence. Their horizon is bounded by those problems which already exist or which can, with a high degree of probability, now be foreseen. Anything else can be left to their successors to take care of. Their immediate concern is to survive, to retain their authority and, by overcoming existing obstacles, to preserve for others the possibility of occupying themselves with problems now only to be guessed at.

Admittedly, even among these actual or imminent problems there are some which assume the form of efforts at international co-operation. On closer examination, however, such phenomena generally turn out to be examples of co-operation for the furtherance of disputes – the North Atlantic Treaty Organization; for the prevention of disputes – the Agreement on the Rescue of Astronauts, the Return of Astronauts and the Return of Objects launched into Outer Space; or for the limitation of disputes – the quadripartite negotiations of 1969 on the Middle East. Others may initially present a more plausibly constructive aspect – the European Economic Community – yet soon engender fresh disputes both among those included in the co-operative effort and, to an even greater extent, with those excluded. If there exist any problems affecting more than one nation-state which are not related to any kind of dispute, whether actual or potential, then these are not problems of international relations as this branch of human activity is commonly interpreted in practice.

Unfortunately the causes, nature and consequences of disputes among nation-states are so various that their identification presents more difficulty than might at first be supposed. Prima facie, a dispute arises whenever objection is manifested by one government to the words, deeds or mere existence of another. For practical purposes, however, the dispute does not usually begin until its existence is recognized by at least two governments. For instance, as soon as the first British traders reached China, the Chinese Government manifested their objection to the existence of any other authority than their own: they made it clear, by word and deed, that they expected all visitors to China, whatever their nationality or status, to conduct themselves in a manner to be determined exclusively by the Chinese Government. This attitude was always resented, often evaded and sometimes actively resisted by the British travellers concerned. Yet this conflict of views between the Chinese Government and individual British travellers did not constitute an international dispute until the British Government decided, after many years, to assert, first by words and subsequently by deeds, that they too were entitled to influence the treatment accorded to their nationals in China. Up to this point whatever happened to British subjects in China was a matter of internal Chinese administration: thereafter it was a matter of international dispute.

The latter contention was not accepted by the Chinese at the time and, when they recognized the existence of a dispute, it was as one stemming solely from piratical British incursions. But agreement on the nature of a dispute – a rare phenomenon – is not essential to the degree of mutual recognition that permits its identification. Moreover, although it is theoretically possible for one government to persist in denying the existence of a dispute asserted by the other, it generally happens that assertions of a dispute are followed by words or deeds that demonstrate its objective reality. When the Chinese Imperial Commissioner concentrated his war junks in the estuary of the Canton River to secure the surrender of a British fugitive, he may or may not sincerely have supposed himself to be conducting a police operation against foreign pirates. When H.M.S. *Volage* and H.M.S. *Hyacinth* opened fire on the Chinese vessels, even he must have realized that a dispute existed, as his government subsequently conceded by their signature of the Treaty of Nanking in 1842.

Nevertheless, although international disputes frequently arise from actions purporting to be within the domestic jurisdiction of one state yet affecting the nationals of another, a positive governmental decision to make this a cause of dispute is always required. Many governments, at different periods, have deliberately avoided such disputes by refusing to interest themselves in the fate of their nationals in other countries or else by forbidding them to travel to particular foreign countries where their treatment might become a source of dispute. Others have gone even further. Between 1939 and 1945, for instance, various European governments successfully avoided disputes by arresting numbers of their own nationals and delivering them to the German Government for enslavement, imprisonment or slaughter. This was naturally as extreme a case as the earlier decision of a British government to fight a war with the ostensible motive of avenging the loss by Captain Jenkins of part of one ear. More ordinary instances can, however, be cited to support the proposition that there are few causes of dispute to which it is in principle impossible to apply the old nursery adage that it takes two to make a quarrel.

Strictly speaking, every manifestation of objection by one government to the conduct of another creates a dispute, but the consequences can naturally be of very unequal importance and duration. The initiating objection is often met, sometimes even anticipated, by apology and redress. When the South African Embassy in London was attacked by rioters in 1969, the Foreign and Commonwealth Office at once expressed regret and promised compensation, so that this potential dispute was still-born. The South African Government might nevertheless have revived it by demanding more extensive redress. Even so, the dispute would not have materialized unless the British Government had manifested their objection by refusing the South African demand or unless British silence or evasion had then been met by South African persistence. Such a dispute, moreover, might assume very different proportions. It might be one of those which intermittently occupy the world's junior diplomats for years, even decades, as they inflate one another's archives by the exchange of routine reminders and acknowledgements, which neither have, nor are expected to produce, any further effect. Or it might grow, slowly or swiftly, into one of those far-reaching crises or devastating wars that have sometimes burgeoned from lesser incidents.

II — DISCRIMINATION AMONG DISPUTES

Historians have devoted a lifetime to analysing the growth of disputes and have seldom accepted one another's explanations. It would thus be idle to pretend that any sure method existed of predicting the likely outcome of disputes still to come. Yet, without some attempt at an approach to this perplexing problem, the practical difficulties inherent in the identification of disputes are in no way resolved by a mere definition or description of this process. Something happens and governments have to decide whether or not to identify this as a cause of dispute by manifesting an objection. If that decision is to be rational, it must be prompted by some prediction of the likely consequences either of declaring a dispute or else of ignoring the incident. Similar considerations apply to a government meditating action but anxious to avoid or anticipate the objections of another government. Neither in theory nor in practice is it possible to argue that certain categories of action will invariably arouse objection and that others will not. Similar causes do not have similar effects in international relations. Nor, even if it can confidently be predicted of a particular action that this will elicit objection from another government, does this constitute a sufficient reason for abstaining from that action. The avoidance of disputes has never been the sole purpose of any government because, in the last resort, disputes are the necessary result of contacts with other governments, just as they are the necessary result of contacts between individual human beings, no two of whom can, when in mutual relations, indefinitely avoid a situation in which their respective purposes are conflicting.

Moreover, once our attention is directed to practical consequences, it must be admitted that the distinction between a dispute and its absence may be less important than the distinction between one kind of dispute and

41

another. Most discussions or negotiations between nation-states could, on close analysis, be shown to relate to disputes. Many of these drag on for decades; some may even be revived after a century of quiescence. But the great majority are either settled or shelved without ever exercising, or even threatening, any significant impact on the lives of the many millions of people who remain entirely unaware either of the existence of the dispute or of the efforts made to solve it. How are these to be distinguished from the small minority that escape from the archives and, transcending the interchange of notes and conversations, find expression in public remonstrance, in acts of retorsion and retaliation, in threats, in the use of force and even in war?

One possible approach to an answer might be to adopt the familiar concept of escalation and to argue that, once an objection is manifested and a dispute thereby identified, a reciprocal process has been initiated which, unless one side or the other terminates it by giving up the dispute or making a concession, has no inherent or obvious limit to its escalation. There would be no difficulty in selecting historical examples, or in constructing theoretical models, to demonstrate how, from its origins in some trivial incident, a dispute may step by step be inflated by the mounting and reciprocal pressures applied by the contestants for the imposition of their own terms until, if both governments and their respective allies maintain their resolution, the world is threatened by the spectre of thermo-nuclear war.

In practice, however, this is not a very helpful approach. Dr. Kahn, games theory and the 'chicken analogy' notwithstanding,[1] it is difficult to think of any past dispute, or to imagine one in the future, conducted as a pure contest in resolve and without regard either to the issues at stake or to the likely consequences. Even the most arrogant, belligerent and intransigent governments do not expect to win every dispute they start and frequently make concessions that can not plausibly be ascribed to mere reluctance to match an act of escalation. The Chinese Government, for instance, are renowned for the readiness with which they engage in disputes and for their tendency to pursue these by acts of violence against the representatives in Peking of the other government concerned. There are probably few other nations capable of matching Chinese escalation in this particular kind of contest. Yet the Chinese have often made concessions to governments whose retaliation they had no reason to fear and whose regard they had no hope of winning. Probably no two Sinologists would agree on the often mysterious reasons for Chinese decisions or succeed in weaving these into a similarly consistent pattern of policy, but it is surely implausible to ascribe the conduct of disputes by this or any other government solely to the desire to demonstrate their own strength and determination. There are always other factors involved, not least an assessment of the intrinsic importance of the issue in dispute.

It would, however, be equally misleading to go to the opposite extreme and to contend that the gravity of a dispute depended on its subject-matter. On 8 June 1967, for instance, the U.S.S. *Liberty*, a naval vessel euphemistically described as a wireless relay ship, was attacked

[1] See Hermann Kahn, *On Escalation* (Praeger 1965).

off the coast of Sinai by Israeli aircraft and torpedo-boats. Damage was inflicted and a number of American sailors were killed or wounded. A similar incident took place on 23 January 1968, when the U.S.S. *Pueblo*, this time admittedly engaged in collecting electronic intelligence off the coast of Korea, was assaulted and captured, together with the crew, by North Korean patrol craft.

Here were two cases in which an American warship had been attacked on what the United States Government contended to be the High Seas by the armed forces of a foreign nation-state. The consequences, however, were very different. The Israeli Government apologized, explained that a mistake had been made and undertook to pay compensation. This dispute ended as swiftly as it had begun. The North Korean Government, on the other hand, immediately aggravated the injury they had inflicted by publicly claiming to have acted in deliberate assertion of their legal rights and, far from offering redress, demanded it. The American Secretary of State thereupon described the ship's seizure as being 'in the category of actions that are to be construed as acts of war' and addressed a formal complaint to a specially convened session of the United Nations Security Council. American words were also reinforced by the recall of reservists, the dispatch of military aircraft to South Korea and a naval demonstration by detachments of the U.S. Seventh Fleet. The dispute was not merely identified but escalated – by both sides, for the North Korean Government threatened and performed acts of violence against their captives.

This discrepancy in the immediate effects of two remarkably similar causes of dispute was also reflected in the ultimate results. Whereas the United States Government received full and prompt satisfaction from Israel, even the release of the *Pueblo*'s crew (the ship and its equipment are still in North Korean hands) could only be obtained by a humiliating, if immediately retracted, American apology and, it was rumoured though later denied, by the payment of a substantial ransom.

The point – and it may seem rather an obvious point – of these two contrasting stories is that the nature of the incident which provokes a dispute does not determine its character, its importance or its subsequent evolution. What does? In these cases it might be argued that the respective attitudes of the Israeli and North Korean governments were decisive. But would American reactions simply have been reversed if the apology from Tel Aviv had been delayed or if one had been forthcoming from Pyongyang? Would the former have galvanized the Sixth Fleet or the latter been immediately accepted?

These may appear naïve questions. Israel is not only in friendly relations with the United States: she is an American protégé, almost a client; North Korea has no diplomatic relations with Washington, she is an unrecognized and ideologically hostile country whose war against the United States has scarcely been more than suspended. Similar causes of offence from such differently situated governments can be expected to elicit different American reactions.

Yet it could not be contended that American responses to an attack against their naval vessels on the High Seas follow automatically from the character of the offending government and the degree of contrition or defiance manifested by the latter. In August 1964, for instance, American destroyers patrolling in the Gulf of Tonking believed themselves to have been attacked by North Vietnamese forces. No damage was caused to either the U.S.S. *Maddox* or the U.S.S. *C. Turner Joy* and some doubt has subsequently arisen about the reality of all the night attacks reported at the time.[1] Yet, although the relationship of North Vietnam to the United States (and to China and the Soviet Union) was substantially the same as that of North Korea in 1968, the American response was not confined to public protests, complaints to the Security Council and naval demonstrations. Actual retaliatory attacks were made – for the first time – against North Vietnamese territory and the dispute thus begun escalated into the most extensive armed conflict fought by the United States since 1945. Yet, in so far as this incident differed from the later attack on the *Pueblo*, both the actions and the words of the North Vietnamese were less provocative and damaging than those of the North Koreans.

If within the short space of four years the same government can react so differently to three such similar causes of objection, further examples would be superfluous to support the proposition that the importance of a dispute can not be assessed merely by the nature of the originating incident or the characteristics of the governments concerned. On the contrary, at this stage in the argument it is necessary to consider the pragmatic retort: that no useful generalization is possible concern-

---

[1] See, for instance: Joseph C. Goulden, *Truth Is The First Casualty*, Rand McNally & Co., Chicago 1969. This book also comments on the *Liberty* and *Pueblo* affairs.

ing disputes, each of which is, and must be, judged entirely in the light of the circumstances in which it arises, of the then state of international relations, of the prevailing intellectual and emotional attitudes of those concerned and of the interaction of their immediate responses. This is a contention of great force and attraction. No two disputes are exactly comparable, nor are the governments involved. Even the United States Government did not have precisely the same outlook, the same set of instinctive responses, in 1964, in 1967 and in 1968. To some extent every new cause of dispute creates a new situation capable of evolving differently from even its most analogous predecessors. International relations will never resemble the physical sciences, where theory can be firmly based on the ability indefinitely to repeat the same practical experiment. In principle it is scarcely possible to refute the pragmatists on this issue: in practice it would be a most inconvenient concession to their views to admit that the fallibility of a theory proved its futility or that the variety of disputes and of their consequences was so great as to elude even the most general and approximate of classifications.

Disputes, after all, are unfortunately frequent. Mr. McNamara calculated[1] that the most dramatic variety – 'internationally significant outbreaks of violence' – were averaging nearly two a month during the sixties. Disputes capable of leading to violence may occur as often as twice a week and there can scarcely be a day in which no official must ask the question: is this a serious dispute, is it urgent, should I get the Minister out of bed or away from his meeting? All these disputes can not possibly

[1] McNamara, op. cit.

47

receive an exhaustively individual assessment before this initial question is answered. The officials of every government must, in practice, rely on certain preconceptions and apply some simple touchstone for their frequent and necessarily hasty acts of discrimination between the important and the routine. It is at least worth inquiring whether this process could be given any theoretical basis more uniform and reliable than the experience and intuition of the particular official concerned.

The purpose of such distinctions and their practical utility need not be confined to the simple question earlier posed: whether or not to disturb the Minister's slumbers? The answer will often be idiosyncratic. It might well be argued, for instance, that the infliction of casualties by an armed attack on an American vessel on the High Seas was always an event requiring the prompt attention of the Secretary of State, even if the circumstances pointed to an early and satisfactory conclusion of the dispute. But this is an argument depending for its force on a known characteristic of the United States Government: their instant accountability to the American Press. It is also subject to an important exception of which the significance will have to be explored at a later stage of the argument: the Secretary of State would not be disturbed if such attacks were so frequent as to have become part of an established pattern, as they were during the Second World War.

Russian officials, on the other hand, need seldom concern themselves with the possibility that the Kremlin will be besieged by the importunate correspondents of *Pravda, Izvestiya* and *Tass*. Yet these officials need to know which disputes their masters will consider important and urgent. In attempting this discrimination they must presumably be guided, as must — for all purposes but that of the immediate Press conference — be their American colleagues, by a prediction of the likely evolution of the dispute. For instance, repeated flights by American reconnaissance aircraft over Soviet territory elicited no significant reaction from the Soviet Government until the day when one of them was shot down. A competent Soviet official might not have been able to guess the exact nature of Mr. Khruschev's dramatization of the resulting dispute, but he should have been able to predict that the character of the objection manifested by the Soviet Government on this occasion was likely to differ significantly from anything elicited by earlier and identical causes of offence. The news of this unexpected break in the pattern does not, however, seem to have prompted any similar prediction in Washington, where the conduct of the first Press conference apparently received more attention than the likely evolution of the U.2 dispute.

Here we encounter, dimly and as yet undefined, the looming presence of ideas later to be examined more thoroughly. There are two kinds of dispute: the routine and the critical, those which can safely be left in the hands of subordinates following their established procedures and those requiring special, urgent, yet considered, attention by the men who take decisions. Most U.2 flights were routine operations by the C.I.A.: this was the cause of an important international crisis which might at least have been mitigated if the potential repercussions of this incident had been understood at an earlier stage in Washington. If somebody, on reading the first agency message, had exclaimed 'this means trouble: hold everything while we think it out', some of the trouble might have been averted.

On what basis might such predictions be made, mere precedent being so obviously misleading, or what, chance combinations of circumstance apart, governs the evolution of disputes? One possible answer, which seems at least to merit exploration, lies in analysis of what might be regarded as the kernel of all disputes: the conflicting motives of the participants. From the standpoint of the official attempting a prediction this conflict of motive may be more precisely defined as that between the purpose for which a dispute was initiated by manifesting an objection, and the intention that prompted the commission of the objectionable act. This distinction between the purpose of one side and the intention of the other is adopted solely for clarity and convenience and has no other significance. It will, however, be retained in the discussion that follows, so that intentions are always attributed to the government committing the objectionable act, purposes to the government manifesting objection. As for the epithet 'objectionable', this simply means capable of arousing objection.

Before its detailed analysis can be attempted, this definition demands some expansion and qualification. The words 'purpose' and 'intention' possess a magnetic attraction for such adjectives as 'good', 'bad', 'sinister', 'disinterested', 'lofty' or 'perfidious'. We shall not be concerned with judgements of this kind, except in so far as these relate to the Apparent aspects of disputes. The assumption underlying the examination which follows is that the way a dispute ends is of greater significance than the way in which it begins. Although superficially an elementary proposition and, in the extreme cases where a dispute ends in violence, an obvious one, this preference for the terminal situation as the criterion for distinguishing one class of dispute from another is not without its practical difficulties. To all but metaphysicians it is relatively easy to define the beginning of a dispute by the manifestation of an objection. But the end of the dispute – the moment when an objection receives sufficient satisfaction, or when it is finally abandoned, or when the dispute it began is so submerged by a new quarrel that the original objection is, for practical purposes, forgotten – this is a boundary seldom susceptible of precise and objective definition even by the historian. To the practising politician or diplomat endeavouring to foresee the likely course of events, the end of the dispute must often appear as shifting and uncertain as the horizon. To ask him to base his initial decisions on a hazy notion of what might eventually come to pass rather than on what has already happened is to ask a great deal.

Yet the concept of a terminal situation is as crucial to the realistic analysis of purposes and intentions as the horizon to the science of navigation. When rational governments manifest an objection, this should not be, and often is not, a mere reflex action: it is meant to achieve something. The deeds or words of another government have given rise to an unsatisfactory state of affairs and the manifestation of objection is the first step towards improving matters. If the end of a dispute leaves the objecting government in a less favourable situation than the beginning, it is often questionable whether the original objection was well judged.

There are naturally exceptions to the concept of ultimate advantage as the touchstone of initial objections. In 1939, for instance, Finland's purpose in resisting Russian territorial demands could not reasonably have been based on the expectation that the end of the dispute would leave Finland in a better position than the beginning. Neither Russian acquiescence nor Finnish military victory were likely terminal situations. On the other hand, it could have been argued that the consequences of initial acceptance of the Russian demands would have been even worse than those of enforced concession after a desperate resistance. In a realistic interpretation of this dispute, therefore, the terminal situation suggested by the presumed intentions of the Soviet Union — to reduce Finland to the condition of Estonia, Latvia and Lithuania — was what had to be avoided. If this assessment of Russian intentions was probable, then the purpose of the Finnish Government was rightly directed, not to the ideal terminal situation, but to the least disadvantageous of those that appeared at all likely. Finland was indeed worse off at the end of the dispute than she had been at the beginning, but not as badly off as she might have been if she had never initiated the dispute at all.

This was a fairly extreme case of the intentions of the opposing government dominating any attempt at decisions in the light of likely terminal situations, whereas the circumstances of the *Liberty* dispute enabled the Government of the United States to regard the terminal situation as one largely to be dictated by their own purposes alone. As a general rule, however, the choice does not lie between the terminal situations indicated, respectively, by the full purposes of one government and the full intentions of another, but has to be qualified by consideration of the will and ability of each to pursue their original aims as the dispute evolves. Prediction, in these circumstances, is a complex and most uncertain task, but even a hazy comparison of the terminal situation which might result from an objection with that which might result from acquiescence in the objectionable act can still prove a more useful guide to decision than an automatic reaction to what may conventionally be considered the intrinsic characteristics of the objectionable act.

When analysing purposes and intentions, therefore, an attempt will be made to discriminate between their Appearance – broadly speaking, the conflicting arguments advanced for and against the intrinsic merits of the objection and of the objectionable act – and their Reality – the terminal situations they can be expected to produce. Metaphysically this is not a readily defensible distinction and it certainly seems to put quite a number of carts before the unfortunate horse. Some of its practical advantages may emerge in the course of argument, but the perplexed and impatient reader may meanwhile be appeased by the reminder that politicians and officials often do approach their problems in this seemingly topsy-turvy manner. The reader of Churchill's *The Gathering Storm*[1] will find that most of the speeches he quotes have, as the core of their argument, a prediction of the eventual outcome of the particular German act to which he would have liked the British Government of the day to manifest a forceful objection. When German troops entered the Rhineland, for instance, what really

[1] Cassell 1948.

concerned Churchill was not the immediate merits of the dispute, but his conception of a terminal situation, in some unspecified but early future, when 'the creation of a line of forts opposite to the French frontier' would enable Germany to threaten 'the Baltic States, Poland and Czechoslovakia, with which must be associated Yugoslavia, Roumania, Austria and some other countries'. The validity of this projection of the dispute naturally depends on his assessment of German intentions, just as certain assumptions concerning British purposes are needed to demonstrate that, if likely, it is also undesirable. Both factors similarly enter into his contrasting picture of the peaceful preservation of the *status quo* through 'the assembly of an overwhelming force' by members of the League of Nations. The importance of this dispute, in Churchill's view, is thus measured by the disparity, in their advantage to Britain, of the different terminal situations it might produce. The Government of the day disagreed with his predictions, but they too based their decision on a comparison of alternative terminal situations: on the one hand a Germany stronger but, her grievance once redressed, less prone to bellicosity; on the other, a war for which Britain was not prepared. Moreover, it was probably only in their prediction of terminal situations that Baldwin and Churchill differed. If asked such questions as 'is German action a breach of international law?' or 'are Hitler's intentions bad?' or even 'is it the purpose of Britain to support France against Germany?' their private opinions would doubtless have coincided.

Illogical though it may seem in principle, and difficult though it undoubtedly is in practice, it is thus by the prediction of terminal situations that the discrimination of disputes is often and, it is here contended, should always be attempted. And, although this process inevitably depends on an assessment of the purposes and intentions of the conflicting governments, the Reality of both can most reliably be inferred from the terminal situations each may be expected to produce. Therefore, in the following examination, first, of the purpose of governments initiating a dispute by the manifestation of an objection and, second, of the intention of governments committing an objectionable act, the distinction sought between Reality and Appearance will be in terms of their ability to contribute to useful prediction.

III — PURPOSES

The most obvious example of this distinction is to be found in the differences suggested by impulse and by rational consideration. The first seeks immediate emotional satisfaction; the second the achievement of concrete results. It would, however, be misleading to equate Apparent purposes with impulsive reactions or to suppose that a considered judgement will necessarily differ. If a man throws a stone at me, my first instinct is to avoid it, but my considered judgement would be the same. This is a problem so simple that, in its initial stage, there is no difference between its Appearance and its Reality. The difficulty arises only when I have to decide what to do next. Whether I rely on instinct or on reason, I have three basic choices: flee, conciliate or fight. In a purely instinctive response my own temperament and the Appearance of the problem — an attack — will be the determining factors. If I pause to think, then my choice depends on my assessment of the situation: what does my assailant intend to do next, how do his resources compare with mine, what is the likely outcome of the various courses of action open to me, which terminal situation do I prefer? It is at this stage that even the coolest and shrewdest of minds may err in their calculations if they have incorrectly apprehended the essence of the problem confronting them. The reaction appropriate to a solitary stone-throwing lunatic, for instance, may prove tragically misplaced if he is a straggler from a large, adjacent and easily incensed mob.

Nevertheless, although the discrepancy between Appearance and Reality may confuse even a reasoned approach to international problems, there is a tendency for emotion to prefer the first and calculation the second. For instance, one explanation of the contrasting American responses to the attacks on the *Liberty* and the *Pueblo* is that the first was promptly disavowed and the second flaunted. In emotional terms, therefore, the first was a regrettable accident and the second a hostile act. This is also a valid description of the Apparent nature of the two incidents, a description which was confirmed by subsequent developments. As an Appearance, however, its validity and significance were independent of any correspondence with objective truth. It is not unknown, for instance, for governments to disavow their agents even when these have acted in exact conformity with undisclosed instructions or, conversely, to uphold them in spite of their blunders. But it would have made no difference if the Israeli Government had been secretly delighted at the enforced withdrawal of the *Liberty* and the North Koreans inwardly appalled by the capture of the *Pueblo*: it is the overt attitude rather than the presumed intentions of the government concerned that determines the Apparent character of an objectionable act.

There is another way of comparing these two incidents. This entails the examination, not of the nature and quality of each objectionable act, but of the concrete situation each had created. This at once reveals one significant contrast: the damaged *Liberty*, her dead and injured still on board, had steamed out of harm's way; the captured *Pueblo*, her crew and her secret equipment were in the hands of the North Koreans and at their mercy. Even without allowing for any divergence in the ultimate intentions of the offending governments, therefore, the factors affecting the purpose of the United States Government in these two disputes differed in a most material respect. In the case of the *Liberty* no American decision – even a decision to do nothing – was likely to make matters worse, unless this decision actually started a fresh dispute. In the case of the *Pueblo* only a correct decision could prevent a still more unsatisfactory situation from developing, as it almost certainly would in the event of American inaction. Although analysis of the Real characteristics of these two disputes thus confirms the initial deduction drawn from their Appearance – that the attack on the *Pueblo* was the more objectionable act of the two – it also reveals this problem as being far more complex and difficult than its mere Appearance – a hostile act – would suggest. In a conventional analysis a deliberately hostile act presents a simpler problem than an accident of ambiguous appearance: realistically, and in practice, the circumstances of the attack on the *Pueblo*, far from clarifying American purposes, actually

57

complicated them by introducing an element of in-compatibility.

On the level of Appearance, where purpose depends on the emotions, instincts or arguments which lead to its formulation in purely subjective terms, this was not a necessary result. The possession of American hostages by the North Korean Government only aggravated the objectionable quality of their original act and strength-ened without complicating the purposes of the United States. Liberating the crew, recapturing the vessel and its secret equipment, restoring American prestige, asserting the right to electronic espionage on the High Seas, upholding international law, securing redress for injury: all these demonstrably desirable goals can be fitted comfortably into a single structure of purpose and, however various the arguments advanced to support each, these need not be mutually inconsistent. Indeed, the more abstract are the criteria by which purposes are defined, the more various and far-reaching these tend to become. On purely ethical principles, for instance, there is no reason to end a dispute before this has resulted in the establishment of the Kingdom of Heaven on Earth.

It is only when the dispute is considered in the light of the preferred terminal situation, that a discrepancy emerges, not only between the order of preference and the order of probability, but also between one practical result and another. If one of the conditions stipulated for the preferred terminal situation is that the crew of the *Pueblo* should return alive to the United States, it at once becomes evident that this result is unlikely without the acquiescence of the North Korean Government. Other possible conditions – further North Korean

ability to offend the United States Government being
eliminated by intensive nuclear bombardment, for instance — are similarly revealed as incompatible with
survival of the crew and also, perhaps, with such other
goals as avoidance of war with the Soviet Union. It thus
becomes necessary to envisage a preferred terminal
situation of which each component is not only individu-
ally attainable but also attainable in combination. In
some cases, as seems to have happened with the *Pueblo*,
a single component will be given priority, so that, in the
event, the United States Government sacrificed most of
their other objectives to ensure the survival and release
of the crew. If this was indeed envisaged from the outset
as the preferred terminal situation (subject, no doubt, to
certain qualifications), there were two obvious methods
of obtaining the necessary degree of co-operation from
the North Korean Government: threats and inducements. Both presuppose that there were terminal situations which that government would either consider more
unwelcome than the liberation of the hostages or else
more desirable than their retention. A rational North
Korean Government, for instance, if convinced that
retention of the hostages would lead to the destruction
of the entire North Korean people, would surely prefer
to release them. The establishment of the necessary
degree of conviction might, however, present some
difficulty. It could have been argued in Pyongyang that
the total destruction of the North Korean people would
necessarily involve that of the hostages as well, but that
any lesser degree of destruction that spared the hostages
would also spare enough Koreans to kill them. Moreover, any serious damage inflicted by the Americans

would carry at least a risk of Russian retaliation against the United States. Therefore, if the United States Government were really giving priority to the liberation of the hostages, they were unlikely to take action that would imperil their own country while simultaneously jeopardizing the very men it was intended to save. On the other hand, if liberation of the hostages were only incidental to the purpose of preventing future interference with electronic espionage, this latter purpose could be just as effectively, though possibly more expensively, achieved by the destruction of North Korea.

An American decision to employ threats thus demanded a prior assessment of the likely North Korean response, which in turn depended on the view taken by the latter of the terminal situation preferred by the United States. Subsequent events suggest that Pyongyang's judgement was better than Washington's. Admittedly the United States Government may deliberately have decided first to try threats and, if these had no effect, only then to resort to inducements. No authoritative account of the motives or calculations of those concerned is yet available.[1] On the other hand, the adverse consequences of allowing one's bluff to be called

---

[1] Some consideration seems to have been given to these points at a fairly early stage:

'There's no reason to believe that the North Koreans would give up the ship and the crew if we bombed them, and in fact they'd be very likely to hang on to them tighter than ever,' theorized one defense planner. 'And there's no reason to believe either that they'll believe us if we just threaten to bomb them,' he added. *Wall Street Journal*, 25 January 1968.

The whole article provides an interesting, and evidently informed, contemporary analysis of the obstacles to any American use of force to secure the release of *Pueblo*'s crew and reveals the importance attached to this purpose from the outset.

are as well known in poker-playing Washington as is the reckless and intransigent nature of the North Korean regime. It is at least possible, therefore, that the initial resort to threats was not prompted by calculation of their likely contribution to a desired terminal situation, but constituted a more or less instinctive response to an objectionable act which, in Mr. Rusk's somewhat cumbrous description, was 'in the category of actions that are to be construed as acts of war'.

This is a most revealing phrase. Mr. Rusk can not possibly have believed that it was the intention of North Korea to make war upon the United States, that this was only the first step — as Churchill predicted of Hitler's reoccupation of the Rhineland — in an ever-widening campaign of aggression that would ultimately threaten the independence of the United States. Such intentions were manifestly beyond the capacity of North Korea. What Mr. Rusk must have meant — as his phraseology suggests — was that actions of this kind could, by historical precedent, in international law, from various ethical standpoints, be regarded as justifying an American resort to war. The intrinsic nature and quality of the act was warlike, hostile and provocative. In other words, Mr. Rusk was initially concerned only with the Apparent nature of the dispute: something had happened that was 'in the category of actions that are to be construed as acts of war', so Mr. Rusk automatically went through the motions of preparing for war. Only afterwards did it become evident that war was unlikely to serve the purpose of the United States, because only afterwards was that purpose defined in the light of the terminal situation it was desired to achieve.

This initial misconception of the problem did not, however, merely lead to delay in the adoption of the measures most appropriate to the attainment of the desired terminal situation. The course of action chosen — the threat of coercion — did more than prolong the dispute: it also ensured that it would ultimately be ended on terms less favourable to the United States than those attainable by other methods. This is an argument which is only partly dependent on hypotheses concerning North Korean reactions. It is not certain, for instance, what the North Korean Government would have done if the United States Government had refrained from all overt acts or public statements and had instead immediately entered into negotiations for the release of the crew. It is conceivable that the North Koreans would then have accepted a less humiliating apology — perhaps for an 'accidental' incursion into their territorial waters — and would have done so much sooner. But, even if negotiations of this kind had elicited exactly the same terms as those ultimately accepted by the United States, this acceptance would have been far less damaging. There would have been no American bluff to be called, no revelation to the watching world that the United States were willing to wound but afraid to strike. Nor would even the apology have seemed so humiliating if it had not been preceded by constant public denials that the *Pueblo* had ever done anything to which exception could legitimately be taken. These were understandable, even desirable, if the United States Government contemplated war or other coercive action needing to be justified to public opinion, but they could only be counterproductive if the terminal situation envisaged was one requiring the co-operation of the North Korean Government.

This over-simplified analysis of a complex problem is not put forward as a criticism of the actual conduct of the United States Government. Before attempting such a judgement it would be necessary to possess a more detailed knowledge of the sequence of events and decisions and to consider carefully the extent to which the options of the United States Government were limited by the exigencies of American domestic politics. Would the actual circumstances of the *Pueblo* incident have allowed President Johnson to follow the example set by President Kennedy in the Cuban crisis of 1962: to devote five days to exhaustive confidential discussion before any public attitude was struck, indeed, before the existence of the problem was even revealed to public opinion? Would this public opinion have allowed the Administration to brush the whole affair under the carpet as an unfortunate mistake to be quickly and quietly settled by an American apology and North Korean release of the crew? Perhaps not, but this theoretical analysis of the *Pueblo* incident nevertheless serves to illustrate the methods by which, in terms of pure foreign policy, the decision to initiate a dispute, the purpose envisaged and the choice of methods for prosecuting the dispute might most efficaciously be arrived at.

This process should, it is suggested, be conducted throughout on the basis of a prediction of terminal situations. The decision to manifest an objection, for instance, should not be prompted by a subjective judgement of the nature and quality of the objectionable act, but by considering what terminal situation could be expected if no objection were manifested. If this hypothetical situation seems undesirable, the next step is to consider the alternatives. This process will usually produce a range of terminal situations, some of them more desirable than others, because some would represent the achievement of more purposes or of purposes regarded as preferable. It is not relevant to the present study to consider why one purpose should be preferred to another. In any given set of circumstances different governments can have very various priorities. All that is here contended is that, if, as usually happens, the objecting government have to choose among several potential purposes, then the right way to choose is to compare the terminal situations which might result from the pursuit of these various purposes. It makes no sense to argue that 'peace' is preferable to 'prestige' or 'prosperity' to either. Abstractions and value judgements have their part to play in deciding which terminal situation is to be preferred, but they are only the tools of comparison, not the objects to be compared, which must be situations capable of description in concrete terms.

This comparison, however, must be directed to feasibility and compatibility as well as to desirability. The most desirable solution – that which fulfils every purpose – must be tested by reference to the cost of its achievement and the will and ability of the opponent to frustrate it. It will generally fail this test, so the desirability of the supposed terminal situation has to be reduced until all its components seem both compatible and possible. This testing of progressively less desirable solutions will, of itself, indicate the choice of methods for their attainment. The whole process is analogous to the method of long division that used to be taught in British schools: when dividing 1463 by 213, one thinks first of 7, but one actually tries 6. Moreover, just as experience teaches the child that, in such a case, it would not even be worth considering 9, so the knowledgeable practitioner of foreign affairs need not waste time in considering the more extreme solutions: he should be able to start with a narrow range of terminal situations, varying from the highly desirable but barely conceivable to the easily attainable but manifestly disadvantageous.

This, it is suggested, is the Realistic approach to defining the purpose with which one government may usefully manifest objection to the conduct of another: not only to avoid the unsatisfactory state of affairs expected to arise in the absence of objection, but also to ensure that the alternative terminal situation is both more favourable and also the most favourable likely to be attainable. In this process one of the first requisites is the ability to assess the intentions of the other party and it is to this difficult question that we must now turn our attention.

IV — INTENTIONS

The importance of assessing the adversary's intentions as part of the process of reaching one's own decisions is widely but not, unfortunately, universally recognized. In *13 Days*[1] the late Senator Robert Kennedy wrote:

> 'The final lesson of the Cuban missile crisis is the importance of placing ourselves in the other country's shoes. During the crisis President Kennedy spent more time trying to determine the effect of a particular course of action on Khruschev or the Russians than on any other phase of what he was doing.'

[1] Robert F. Kennedy, 13 *Days* (Macmillan 1969).

Robert Kennedy also comments, however, on the President's distress that so many of the American military and naval officers consulted during the crisis:

> 'seemed to give so little consideration to the implications of the steps they suggested. They seemed always to assume that the Russians and the Cubans would not respond or, if they did, that a war was in our national interest.'

This failure to consider the likely intentions of the adversary need not have been the result of mere intellectual laziness: it could equally well have been rooted in scepticism as to the possibility of reaching any assessment sufficiently reliable to offer a useful guide to decision. After all, at the outset of his story, Robert Kennedy records the dominant reaction to the identification of missile sites in Cuba as having been one of 'shocked incredulity', because the United States Intelligence Board had earlier concluded that the Soviet Government did not intend to install missiles in Cuba or anywhere else beyond the borders of the Soviet Union. The complete falsification by events – and that within a mere four weeks – of this carefully considered and expert opinion may well have fortified believers in that well-established maxim – often endorsed by Harold Nicolson:

> 'Not to worry about what the other man might have at the back of his head, but to make quite sure that he was in no doubt regarding the certainty of your own intentions.'[1]

If both Khruschev and Kennedy had been guided exclusively by that maxim in October 1962, it is unlikely

[1] Harold Nicolson, *Curzon: The Last Phase*, Chapter II (Constable 1934).

that these words would now be written or that they would find many readers in the northern hemisphere. Whenever the adversary is capable of having more than one intention and whenever the results to be expected from his choice of intentions offer contrasting degrees of advantage, it must always be of importance to guess which of his various possible intentions he is more likely to act on. And the contingency of an opponent with only one option or with a range of options incapable of producing significant differences in the terminal situation is too rare to merit consideration. Robert Kennedy quotes an illuminating example of what might, on a first and superficial examination, have been considered such a contingency:

'I remember an earlier meeting on Laos, in 1961, when the military unanimously recommended sending in substantial numbers of United States troops to stabilize the country. They were to be brought in through two airports with limited capability. Someone questioned what we would do if only a limited number landed and then the Communist Pathet Lao knocked out the airports and proceeded to attack our troops, limited in number and not completely equipped. The representatives of the military said we would then have to destroy Hanoi and possibly use nuclear weapons. President Kennedy did not send in troops. . . .'[1]

These are mostly examples of tactical or immediate intentions. If a particular move is made by one government, what response can be expected from the other and how would this response differ if the move made by the first government was different? Such questions are customarily answered by considering the range of options

[1] Kennedy, op. cit.

within the capacity of the other government and the preferences which previous experience suggests as characteristic of their conduct. But it is also necessary to take into account the strategic or long-term intentions of the other government. These are equally important before the dispute begins – when an assessment of intentions is needed to help determine the significance of the objectionable act – and during the dispute, when likely responses can scarcely be predicted without reference to the pattern of intention in which these responses are only components. In the attacks on the *Maddox*, the *Liberty* and the *Pueblo*, for instance, the ultimate intentions of the three governments concerned were clearly relevant to any assessment of their immediate intentions in committing these identically objectionable acts. Similarly, if the United States Government had in each case taken identical action – dispatched a diplomatic note demanding compensation, for example – no reliable prediction of the response could have been made without regard to the strategic intentions of the offending governments.

These intentions can be described in different ways. One of these is by the attribution of motives, which are then distinguished as 'good' or 'bad' or by some equivalent of these epithets. In October 1962, for instance, Khruschev said he had sent missiles to Cuba 'to strengthen its defensive potential', whereas President Kennedy described the Russian action as 'an explicit threat to the peace and security of all the Americas'. We need not waste any time in arguing which of these descriptions was more nearly correct. It makes no difference. Whether Russian aims were defensive or offensive, whether the former could be justified and the latter could not, whether Mr. Gromyko actually lied when he told President Kennedy that only 'defensive' arms had been sent to Cuba: all these are questions for the school-men. Just as the only reliable distinction between offensive and defensive weapons is the direction in which these are pointed, so the only worth-while criterion of intentions is the terminal situation these may be expected to produce.

In the Cuban crisis this terminal situation was clearly and objectively defined in President Kennedy's speech of 22 October 1962: 'a nuclear strike capability against the Western Hemisphere.' Other passages in the same speech may, it has subsequently been alleged, have exaggerated the number and range of the missiles con-cerned, just as some of the more moralistic arguments employed are open to challenge. But on the central issue no reasonable doubt exists: missiles had been introduced into Cuba for which the only plausible targets were on the territory of the United States and of their allies. If no objection was manifested by the United States Government, the installation of these missiles would be completed and the terminal situation – 'a nuclear strike capability against the Western Hemisphere' – would be more disadvantageous to the United States than the continued presence of these missiles in the Soviet Union itself, whence they would have been unable to reach the United States.

This was a Real cause of dispute, in which Soviet intentions (no matter whether these were offensive or defensive, legitimate or not – the impact of a legitimate, defensive thermo-nuclear explosion is no different from any other) could be reliably assessed from the terminal situation which their concrete acts would inevitably produce. Nor did prediction of this particular terminal situation demand any consideration of the longer-term intentions of the Soviet Government, though these would be an important element in the next stage of analysis: ascertaining whether there existed alternative terminal situations which were both feasible and less disadvantageous. It was to this process, fortunately for the human race, that the United States Government devoted five days of intensive discussion from Tuesday 16 October to Saturday 20 October 1962. The progress of their deliberations may be followed in Kennedy's *13 Days* and, in greater detail, in Abel's enthralling *The Missiles of October*.[1]

The aspect which immediately concerns us is American assessment of Russian intentions. That the Russians wanted a nuclear strike capability in Cuba was obvious. The legitimacy of their motives in wanting it was irrelevant, but it was vital to be able to predict which alternative terminal situations the Soviet Government might be prepared to contemplate. Here a most material factor was that the missiles had been discovered before they were ready for use. During these critical five days, therefore, the American planners knew that the problem as seen from Moscow was about to undergo a major change. What the Russians had presumably envisaged as the optimum terminal situation – confronting the Americans with the *fait accompli* of a nuclear strike capacity in Cuba – was no longer possible. Once the United States Government revealed their knowledge,

[1] Elie Abel, *The Missiles of October* (MacGibbon & Kee 1966).

the Soviet Government would have to consider other possibilities, if, indeed, they had not done so already. That their preferences would include immediate war was inherently unlikely. If they had run the risks (depriving themselves temporarily of part of their striking force and impairing the chances of surprise) inseparable from sending so many missiles to Cuba, it was presumably because they expected substantial military advantage from a completed nuclear strike capacity in Cuba. Without this capacity they were actually worse placed than before, because they had alerted the Americans and deprived themselves of a number of missiles which could have been employed against American bases in Europe. From the purely military standpoint, therefore, the arguments against war would surely seem stronger at this anticlimax than they were before the operation had ever begun and the Russians would thus be more inclined to consider an alternative terminal situation. The danger, however, was that they might either hope for a solution more favourable than the United States could permit – being able to complete the installation of their missiles, for instance – or else despair of American acquiescence in any solution not entailing for the Soviet Government an unacceptable loss of prestige and even authority.

This was a danger fully realized by President Kennedy, who took as much trouble to preserve the Russian line of retreat as he did to bar their further advance. His policy was so successful that the dispute was terminated in a manner that both governments were able to regard as advantageous. In the United States, admittedly, Khruschev's subsequent claim to the achievement of preventing an American invasion[1] has generally been regarded as the mere rationalization of defeat. In a phrase most inconsistent with President Kennedy's instructions that no statement should be made claiming any kind of victory, Mr. Rusk later declared that: 'we looked into the mouth of the cannon; the Russians flinched.' As Mr. Macmillan has sensibly commented: 'perhaps it was not quite so simple as that.'[2]

Russian secrecy is such that we may never know the truth of this strange and perilous episode. Nevertheless, in 1962 it was not an unreasonable Russian hypothesis that the United States intended to invade Cuba and overthrow the Castro regime. If this seemed to the Soviet Government undesirable, it is not obvious how else they could have expected to prevent it except by the threat of nuclear war or what better measures they could have adopted to make such a threat credible. It is conceivable, therefore, that the terminal situation throughout envisaged by the Soviet Union was one in which Cuba was free from the threat of American invasion, because the United States had realized that this would involve the risk of nuclear war. From the Russian point of view this immunity might be best assured by the presence of a Russian nuclear strike capacity on Cuban soil, but it is not impossible that the idea of an American promise extorted under the threat of nuclear war had

[1] 'There were people who began to criticize us for placing the missiles and then taking them away. It is true we did emplace them and removed them. But we received the promise that there would be no invasion of Cuba.' N. S. Khruschev – speech of 17 January 1964 – quoted in Thomas W. Wolfe, *Soviet Strategy at the Crossroads* (Harvard University Press 1964).

[2] Kennedy, op. cit., Preface.

been considered, even before the operation began, as a second best. This may seem an extravagant hypothesis[1] – that the Russians should ever have considered emulating the grand old Duke of York to the extent of shipping missiles to Cuba only to bring them away again. Precedents, however, are not lacking. Nicolson refers contemptuously to 'the old Geiseltheorie of Holstein – the theory that it is a clever diplomatic move to seize some pledge or "Faustpfand" and to refuse to surrender it except in return for payment'.[2] Nicolson has no difficulty in demonstrating the failure of this expedient in the Agadir crisis of 1911, but it has not always been unsuccessfully attempted, nor was the Cuban crisis of 1962 the first occasion on which such ideas had been attributed to the Soviet Government.

The main interest of this essentially unverifiable speculation is that it offers a rational explanation of Russian conduct and the entire theory here advanced depends on the assumption that, as a general rule, governments do act rationally. It also helps to explain what was earlier noted as a significant deterrent to any reliance on analysis of the adversary's intentions as a guide to understanding the Real nature of disputes: the prediction by the United States Intelligence Board that the Soviet Government did not intend to install missiles in Cuba or anywhere else beyond the frontiers of the

[1] The case against it has been plausibly argued by Horelick and Rush in 'Strategic Power and Soviet Foreign Policy', but their thesis – 'the object of this manœuvre was not, as in Berlin, to use Soviet strategic power directly to force local concessions but rather to exact political concessions in Berlin and elsewhere' – assumes a degree of Soviet confidence in the full success of their manœuvre much at variance with the same authors' assessment of habitual Soviet caution.

[2] Harold Nicolson, *Lord Carnock*, Chapter 12 (op. cit.).

Soviet Union. This seems – neither Kennedy nor Abel provide particulars of the supporting arguments – to have been a prediction based on precedent and considerations of military advantage. Both were surely insufficient, because Cuba was an exceptional case in 1962: the only Communist country incapable of conventional defence against the likely weight of conventional attack. If its defence was necessary, therefore, only nuclear weapons would suffice. Admittedly the nuclear deterrent existed within the Soviet Union itself, but even the Soviet leaders must have been conscious of how often their previous threats had, for want of performance, diminished the conviction carried by those that followed. If the Americans intended to invade Cuba, more than words would be needed to deter them. Perhaps the United States Intelligence Board failed to perceive this logical argument because they were unable to accept the idea of Russian belief in the aggressive intentions of the United States. If so, their coverage of the American Press must have been inadequate.

It would, however, be misleading to present the Cuban missile crisis merely as a dangerous dispute peacefully resolved by agreement on a mutually acceptable terminal situation. It is true that many of the American deliberations – and only these have been revealed to us – did turn on the crucial concepts of purposes, intentions and terminal situations. It is conceivable that similar mental processes occurred in the Kremlin. But there is also evidence that the Apparent aspects of the dispute exercised considerable influence. President Kennedy's famous broadcast speech of 22 October 1962, for instance, repeatedly employed such phrases as 'deliberate deception', 'a cloak of secrecy and deception', 'this sudden clandestine decision'. Yet he would have been the first to repudiate the notion that the installation of a Russian nuclear strike capacity in Cuba would have been any more acceptable to the United States if it had been announced in advance on Moscow Radio. Similarly, Robert Kennedy says 'we spent more time on this moral question during the first five days than on any other single matter' – the moral question being whether the 'moral position at home and around the globe' of the United States could survive an American surprise attack on Cuba.[1] In retrospect this seems an almost inconceivable dilemma. Even if we suppose that the American leaders did not regard the Bay of Pigs affair of the previous year as constituting an American surprise attack on Cuba, the question at issue was surely whether any attack on Cuba, surprise or otherwise, would provoke a nuclear war. If it did, then the moral position of the United States would be supremely irrelevant. At first sight the importance attached by the two Kennedys to the element of surprise (whether in Russian actions or American proposals) seems to be one of the emotional legacies of American mythology concerning the Japanese attack on Pearl Harbor in 1941. The context of these references also makes it clear that both were thinking of the Apparent aspects of the dispute. Yet, as we shall see later, the concept of surprise possesses a Real significance which they may perhaps have intuitively

---

[1] Kennedy, op. cit. If this statement is to be reconciled with the first quotation on page 63, then the President, fortunately for us all, had a greater sense of the reality of the dispute than his advisers.

perceived, even if their formulation lacked any objective validity.

On balance, however, and without regard to this last hypothesis, the Cuban crisis of 1962 may not unreasonably be regarded as one in which the basic theme of Reality, the choice of terminal situations according to the desirability indicated by one's own purposes and the possibility suggested by the presumed intentions of the opponent, eventually triumphed over all the discordant variations introduced by arguments about the Apparent aspects of the dispute. It was not, however, an easy triumph and neither the accounts that have so far appeared of American deliberations, nor the conclusions seemingly drawn by such responsible American statesmen as Mr. Rusk permit much optimism about the outcome of future disputes of comparable gravity. Some lessons were clearly drawn by the Super-Powers from the stark drama of that confrontation, yet each succeeding year has borne its bitter crop of decisions taken in haste and repented at leisure. In May 1967, for instance, it is hard to discern much regard for terminal situations in the conduct of any non-Israeli statesman during the complex and still largely unexplained manœuvres by many governments that were to precipitate the Six Day War. It is accordingly worth emphasizing, even though this is little more than a recapitulation of earlier arguments concerning purposes, that any assessment of the adversary's intentions must be related to the terminal situations these can reasonably be expected to produce either in the absence of objection or as a result of different kinds of objection. Merely to stigmatize these intentions as evil is unhelpful: it goes without saying that, in any dispute, the other side is wrong and we are right. What matters is to identify the least disadvantageous terminal situation which, in the light of his known capacities and presumed intentions, the adversary can be induced to accept. This difficult process was successfully accomplished by President Kennedy: it does not seem even to have been attempted by President Nasser or by many other leaders lacking his emotional excuse for their neglect.

It is arguable, of course, that none of the erroneous decisions taken in this and other crises were preceded by such prolonged and intensive discussions as those described by Robert Kennedy. He argues convincingly that less correct and far more dangerous choices might have been made in October 1962 if these had not been debated at length, in secrecy and in exhaustive detail among a group of men with sharply conflicting views. His account of the time and effort devoted to this process by the principal American leaders and their widely chosen advisers is deeply impressive and deserves careful consideration by all advocates of the convenience of the quick decisions that emanate from a small group of like-minded men. These five days of agonized and unremitting debate contrast sharply, not least in their eventual results, with the somnambulism that seemed to afflict the rulers of Europe as, washing their hands, they made their automatic and scarcely argued responses to the successive stimuli that began on 23 July 1914 with the Austrian ultimatum.

It is, however, obvious that every dispute can not receive similar treatment: the machinery of government as this operates in most of the capitals of the world would not survive such constant strain. Naturally this machinery could, and should, be improved. A misplaced zeal for economy often requires disputes to be considered by officials preoccupied by problems of lesser importance but, judged by the standards of domestic politics and bureaucratic routine, of equal urgency. There would be a truer cost-efficiency in maintaining a separate Crisis Team of picked (and not for their orthodoxy) officials exempt from routine responsibilities but devoted to the analysis, as it arose, of each fresh dispute and able, if this threatened to assume serious proportions, to give to its handling their undivided attention. Even so, the decision that a particular dispute demanded the attention of the Team and, a more crucial factor, that it required the diversion from their normal preoccupations of some of those key leaders whose rôle could less readily be duplicated, would demand a high degree of judgement. If the Crisis button were pressed too early, it would often be pressed unnecessarily and the whole system would fall into disrepute and, consequently, into disuse. But, if the decision were deferred until the importance of the dispute was obvious, it might then be too late for the Team to take over. Whatever system is adopted to ensure that important disputes receive the thorough and undivided attention they deserve must necessarily depend on the ability to detect these disputes at an early stage, hence to discriminate between the implications of one objectionable act and another.

Occasionally these objectionable acts seem to speak for themselves, as did the arrival of Russian nuclear missiles in Cuba, though even here Robert Kennedy records the existence of 'a small minority, who felt the missiles did not alter the balance of power and therefore necessitated no action'.[1] On the other hand, few of the world's statesmen would have disagreed with the view expressed on 30 June 1914 by the Permanent Under-Secretary of the Foreign Office: 'the tragedy which has recently occurred at Sarajevo will, I hope, not lead to any further complications.'[2] At the dramatic outset of two of the world's most dangerous disputes there were men of great experience and exceptional access to information who yet failed to foresee developments and implications that hindsight has made obvious. Is there any hope that theory could offer a pointer capable of assisting, to however slight an extent, their successors to avoid similar errors? If so, what might that touch-stone be?

It would not, of course, be a substitute for a thorough examination of the purposes and intentions of the con-testants in the light of the terminal situations these might produce. Nothing can replace that process. What we are now seeking is what the intelligence experts call an 'indicator', a specific symptom that would at least suggest the advisability of devoting to the emerging dispute, and from the outset, that exhaustive and undivided attention which, as we have already seen, is likely in present circumstances to constitute an exceptional response. When objectionable acts are committed, for instance, are there any characteristics of which the presence would automatically suggest the need for immediate and thorough analysis of the likely intentions of the govern-ment concerned?

[1] Kennedy, op. cit.
[2] Nicolson, *Lord Carnock*, op. cit.

This is a question that conceals two important assumptions. The first of these has already been expounded: that the importance of a dispute resides in its end rather than its beginning. The kind of dispute for which an indicator is needed is the kind which is likely to confront governments with violence as one of their possible options. The second assumption is that the full implications of many objectionable acts are not immediately apparent. To revert to an earlier analogy: when a man throws a stone at me, analysis is unnecessary; when he picks up a stone or throws one at someone else, his action may or may not also be significant to me and deserve my consideration. The existence of ambiguity, and the consequent need for indicators as an aid to discerning the intentions behind the actions of the adversary, are already widely accepted in military problems: when it is necessary to distinguish between manœuvres intended only to train the troops and those that constitute a disguised mobilization preparatory to a surprise attack. In such cases the Appearance – the number of troops, their location, the wording of any official announcement – may all be less significant to the expert than such minor and sometimes seemingly un-military symptoms as alterations to the railway time-tables or efforts to expedite the harvest. These indicators are all actions which, in the view of the intelligence expert, the adversary would have to take before embarking on actual military operations, but which he would probably omit when carrying out routine training or making a mere show of force. Both singly and in their combination these indicators have to be chosen differently for each country to which they are applied and their utility is obviously greater in predicting a conventional invasion than a nuclear strike.

We shall not, however, be concerned with the use of military indicators as an aid to political prediction or even with an attempt to devise political indicators applicable to particular countries. Both are obviously relevant to the task of prediction, but both are subjects for separate and much more detailed study. What is at issue here is whether there exists any generally applicable symptom capable of suggesting that an otherwise ambiguous objectionable act is likely to provoke a crisis rather than a mere dispute.

V — CHANGE AS THE CRITERION

One possible answer, which may deserve further examination, seems to emerge from President Kennedy's historic and very carefully composed speech of 22 October 1962 on the Cuban crisis. This not only expounded his views on the nature of that particular dispute and sought to justify the policy he had adopted, but also put forward certain principles of avowedly more general application. Some of these manifestly relate only to the Apparent aspects of disputes. For instance, the remark that 'neither the United States of America nor the world community of nations can tolerate deliberate deception and offensive threats on the part of any nation, large or small'[1] is simply untrue. Conduct of this kind has repeatedly been not only tolerated, but practised, by most members of 'the world community of nations', including the United States. Even the more specific statement that any substantially increased possibility of the use of

[1] Kennedy, op. cit.

nuclear weapons or any sudden change in their deployment 'may well be regarded as a definite threat to peace' would need considerable qualification to explain the absence of crisis accompanying the many substantially increased possibilities achieved at one time or another by all the nuclear powers, to say nothing of the secret movements of American missile submarines. We may equally disregard references to 'aggressive conduct', 'course of world domination', 'Soviet threat to peace' and similar rhetorical equivalents of the phrase 'an objectionable act'. What we are seeking is a general statement as neutral and precise as the President's definition of the particular intention of the Soviet Union:

> 'to provide a nuclear strike capability against the Western Hemisphere.'[1]

Such a statement can, in fact, be isolated from the very core of the speech:

> 'I call upon Chairman Khruschev to halt and eliminate this clandestine, reckless and provocative threat to world peace and to stable relations between our two nations.'

If the purely emotive words are discarded, we are left with a concept that could actually be employed in most disputes and by both sides: 'threat . . . to stable relations between our two nations.' The key is the adjective: not 'good', 'friendly', 'peaceful' or even 'mutually respectful', but 'stable'. The relations between any pair of states are not only intrinsically various, but can be very differently described by each of them. That between the

[1] For this and other quotations from the speech, see Kennedy, op. cit.

Soviet Union and Czechoslovakia, for instance, was scarcely susceptible of agreed definition by persons of markedly different political preconceptions between 1950 and 1967. But, in Moscow, Prague or Washington, most people would probably agree that this relationship was stable during those seventeen years and that, during 1968, it became unstable.

The choice of this example does not, of course, imply identification of stability with any degree of alliance or subordination. An aloof and hostile relationship can be just as stable as one of intimate co-operation. The essence of stability in any relationship is predictability. The last few years have not diminished the mutual hostility of the United States and the Soviet Union, but the stability of their relationship has increased – perhaps as one of the results of the Cuban crisis – because both governments have come to accept that, for the time being, the risks of any attempt to impose a major change in the established pattern of this peculiar relationship would outweigh any likely advantage. Ideological considerations and mutual distrust would make it difficult for either to enter into an express agreement to preserve the *status quo*, but both have in practice tended to conduct themselves as if they wished to manifest their tacit and provisional acceptance of limitations on the extent and pace of tolerable change. In so doing each has developed a pattern of behaviour increasingly recognized by the other as predictable, a factor to which both governments attach obvious importance. Against this background of predictability even apparent breaks in the pattern can sometimes be more easily explained between Americans and Russians than between peoples sundered by no similar gulf of mutual antipathy and distrust. The American denial that their aircraft had bombed Egypt in June 1967 was instantly, if tacitly, accepted in Communist Moscow, but not in Capitalist Beirut. Similarly the Russian repudiation of any intentions beyond the restoration of their control in Czechoslovakia seems to have found immediate credence in Washington in August 1968. Indeed, the coolness of official American reactions to the invasion of Czechoslovakia slightly shocked those Europeans whose attention had been concentrated on the Apparent aspects of this incident rather than on its Reality in terms of Soviet-American relations.

Some commentators, however, attach less importance to stability than to predictability, which they treat as a function of the ability to communicate and to establish mutual comprehension. This theory has its attractions. As thermo-nuclear Super-Powers the United States and the Soviet Union inevitably possess a fund of shared knowledge and experience denied to the governments of many lesser states. Even without resort to such devices as the 'hot line', it may sometimes be easier for an American official to divine the mental processes of a Russian than for either to comprehend an Arab. In the modern world there are more political virgins than the domestic conduct of those concerned might suggest.

It may nevertheless be doubted whether this is really the crucial factor. The relationship between China and the United States, for instance, has been conducted with something approaching a minimum of communication or mutual comprehension – let alone good will – during the last decade. Yet the two governments have fallen into a pattern of mutual self-restraint that has given them a relationship more stable and punctuated by fewer conflicts or crises than that obtaining during the same period between China and the Soviet Union. There are few people with whom the Chinese are better equipped to communicate than the Russians, few with whom they share a greater fund of common knowledge and experience. Yet, in 1969, the Chinese and Soviet governments probably regarded each other as being less predictable and hence more immediately dangerous than the United States – for each of them apparently the supreme enemy. Indeed, on the level of Appearance the most grievous offence each lays to the charge of the other is that of secret alliance with the United States: in Reality Chinese and Russian soldiers have fought one another and not the Americans.

At any given moment there is a certain pattern in the relationships of different states. Their intercourse is governed by tacit conventions depending on the view each forms of the type of conduct to be expected from the other. As long as these conventions are maintained, disputes seldom attain serious proportions, because each contestant regards the intentions of the other as likely to fall short of fundamental change in their existing relationship. But, once the pattern is broken and the actions of one state suggest intentions that are unpredictable, so will be the reactions of others.

One of the curious phenomena of the present age, for instance, is the seeming lack of any causal and directly proportionate link between acts of violence and international crises. As these words are written, human beings are being killed in the Middle East, in Nigeria and in Vietnam. In each case foreign governments, including at least one of the Super-Powers, are involved, whether as direct participants or as the suppliers of advice, arms and technical assistance. Yet — such is the horrifying paradox of our times — these have almost become stable situations. As the casualties in Vietnam have risen, so the risk of wider repercussions has diminished. In earlier — and less bloody — phases of that conflict, China, the Soviet Union and the United States were mutually uncertain of the extent of one another's intentions. Now there is tacit acceptance that the conflict will be confined within limits that threaten no change in the existing pattern of their relations. In the brief lull that followed the Israeli victory of June 1967 there was a similar risk of misunderstanding between the Soviet Union and the United States. Once it was established that neither intended to destroy the protégés of the other, that risk was eliminated, nor was it revived by the daily Arab-Israeli clashes of 1969. The sufferings of the Nigerian people today are worse than those of the Congolese in the early sixties, but far less a subject of international dispute and potential conflict among outside governments accepting that the intentions of their rivals are limited this side of any fundamental change in international relationships.

This may not seem a very consoling or even important thought to those directly involved in the fighting, but it is obviously relevant to our examination of ambiguously objectionable acts, which naturally allow greater scope for divergent interpretation when they are directed against a third party.

Before subjecting this notion to further examination,

however, it is necessary to define it rather more precisely and, to that end, briefly to recapitulate the earlier phases of the argument. This began with the proposition that the solution of international problems depended on a clear comprehension of their Real, as opposed to their Apparent, nature. These problems were then defined as disputes arising when objection was manifested by one government to the conduct of another. Such disputes, however, were of very unequal importance and their consequences bore no necessary relation to the nature of the original objectionable act or to the character and circumstances of the governments concerned. To discover some means of discriminating between disputes it accordingly became essential to consider the purposes for which governments manifested objection to the conduct of others. This produced the concept of a terminal situation: a state of affairs more advantageous to the objecting government than anything to be expected in the absence of an objection. This concept depended on a comparison of the purposes, and resources, of one government with the intentions and resources of another, a process shown by the example of the Cuban crisis to be one of great difficulty and to demand an exceptional concentration of intellectual effort and knowledge. International disputes being so frequent there was a risk that the exertions required for a satisfactory analysis of their likely terminal situations would, even with a much improved governmental organization, often be undertaken too late to avoid the Real nature of the dispute being distorted by hasty reactions to its Apparent aspects. Such distortions were naturally always undesirable, but, as was shown by the example of the Cuban crisis, could also prove extremely dangerous. It thus seemed useful, particularly in those disputes of which the critical character might not otherwise have been immediately obvious, to look for some special feature which, when it accompanied an objectionable act, would indicate the need for exceptional care.

It is against this background that we might now attempt a formulation in terms acceptable to both parties in most disputes.

Whenever the immediate consequences of an objectionable act, or the intention to be inferred from its commission, would entail a change in the established pattern of an international relationship, there is a threat of instability, and hence of crisis, proportional to the pace, extent and unexpected character of the change.

It will, of course, at once be remarked that this indicator for the analysis of terminal situations is itself based on an initial prediction: the consequences to be expected either from the act itself or from the intentions which presumably prompted it. The test to be applied thus operates only at one remove: it is not concerned with the intrinsic nature and quality either of the act itself or of the intentions behind it.

The inevitability of this complication may be demonstrated by analysis of an apparent exception, an extreme case in which the existence of a potential crisis could arguably be diagnosed from the mere nature and quality of the initiating event: the impact of a thermo-nuclear missile on American soil. It can scarcely be doubted that this would receive the full emergency treatment and that, as happened when President Kennedy was assassinated, American forces throughout the world would be alerted and American leaders and experts mobilized for the task of analysis. But why? Not because of the extent of the death and destruction: even a missile that exploded almost harmlessly in the middle of the Nevada desert would be a cause of international crisis, whereas a major earthquake that killed quarter of a million people in San Francisco would not. Moralists might argue that the distinction lay in the potentially wrongful nature of the act: that an earthquake could never imply any degree of human, let alone alien, guilt. On this assumption the gravity of the resulting crisis could be predicted on a culpability scale from the zero of accidental release from an American base to the maximum of deliberate discharge from a Russian.

In practice the problem would be less simple. Even if, as might well happen, the first news received by the President of the United States was a telephone call from the commander of the American missile base reporting the inadvertent release of one of his weapons, this would not eliminate the risk of an international crisis. It would merely alter its nature, in that the objectionable act would have been committed by the United States. This may seem a surprising description of accidental damage confined to American nationals and territory. As seen from Moscow, however, the position would be that an American missile aimed at the Soviet Union had fallen short. Either this had been prematurely released in the course of preparations for a larger attack — and a prudent President would not wait many minutes before getting on the hot line to deny any such intention — or else the threat to the Soviet Union posed by the targeting of American missiles was more acutely dangerous, because less stable and predictable, than previously supposed. Indeed, if the suspicions long entertained by laymen concerning the fallibility of ballistic missiles were ever to receive such dramatic confirmation, objections might be expected from more governments than that of the Soviet Union. All concerned would ask themselves, not whether the Americans were morally guilty or innocent, but whether this incident called in question what had previously been assumed to be the essentially stable character of the balance of nuclear terror.

This is not to say that such an incident would necessarily result in a grave international crisis: merely that its potentialities would from the outset demand exceptional treatment because of its departure from the established pattern whereby the United States and the Soviet Union point missiles at one another, but do not suddenly fire them off. The danger of a crisis would admittedly be greater if numerous American casualties were inflicted by a missile of Russian origin (or vice versa): no statesman can hope to be entirely immune from emotional reactions, whether his own or those of his followers. But, in a Realistic analysis, the difference would be one of degree rather than of kind and the response ought still to be determined by an estimate of the adversary's intentions rather than of his culpability. A man who deliberately points a loaded weapon at another can never claim moral innocence if death results, but, when the cost of punishing the guilty may have to be counted in megadeaths, a comparison of likely terminal situations offers a better guide to decision than ethical principles. Ascertaining (probably an impossible task) the precise degree of guilty intent behind the discharge of that first missile would be much less urgent and important than guessing what actions might most easily provoke, or deter, the discharge of the thousands still remaining. To this end it would be essential for each side to determine whether the other now wished to return to the stable relationship momentarily disrupted by the explosion.

Here even the most tolerant of readers may be impelled to protest. If nuclear missiles explode, if Russian rockets are shipped to Cuba, if Egyptian tanks mass in the Sinai desert, what need is there for such sophisticated, such abstract, such tortuous theories as that of a potential threat to the stability of international relations? If a man points a gun at me, no arguments are needed to convince me of the existence of a crisis. What is wrong with the old concept of the threatening or offensive or warlike act?

What is wrong with it is the mid-twentieth century, when most of us must spend our lives under the menace of unseen weapons and only a minority of the human race can have much confidence of being immune from annihilation at five minutes notice. Anyone in the potential target areas (and how many of us are outside?) of the various nuclear powers, is the daily victim of the most threatening, offensive and warlike act yet devised. Even those who flatter themselves that they are low on the list of nuclear priorities may daily be exposed to other dangers. Many millions have come to regard warlike acts as part of the normal routine of their existence. Fighting has been endemic in large areas of the world for decades and now seems so normal that, not long ago, British and Indonesian soldiers fought each other for three years without either government finding it necessary to interrupt diplomatic relations. This century has seen just twelve months in which British troops were not in action somewhere in the world, but neither the British Government, nor other governments often far more deeply involved in hostilities, seem to have found it appropriate to declare a single war since 1945. Any concept that assumes a clear distinction between peace and war, between normal and abnormal behaviour, between good and bad intentions, is simply out of date. A complex age regrettably demands more complicated formulae.

It may nevertheless freely be conceded that, in many disputes, decisions will be based on other arguments. In May 1967 few Israelis would have cared whether President Nasser intended to introduce an element of instability into the pattern of limited and indirect hostility that had characterized the previous decade: the movement of his tanks seemed to speak for itself. The indicator offered by the threat of instability is only likely to be accepted as useful and necessary in those situations where simpler forms of menace are either less obviously apparent or else have become a permanent feature of everyday life. But, to establish its reliability in these circumstances, it has been necessary to show that it also applies, however superfluously, to more blatant crises.

It is, after all, the exception rather than the rule for a grave crisis to manifest its existence beyond all doubt at the very outset of a dispute. In the past, no less than today, serious conflicts have grown from small beginnings, sometimes from an accumulation of intrinsically ambivalent incidents. In 1914, for instance, it took the British Government — and those members of the German Government who were opposed to general war — a fatal month to realize that the assassination at Sarajevo had triggered a major crisis. Determinists have subsequently argued that this delay hardly mattered: war was the inevitable outcome of rivalries among the Great Powers, of their accumulated armaments and of their mobilization plans. For years the forces of mutual destruction had been so piled up that, once the Archduke's murder had started the first slide, nothing could have arrested the avalanche that inevitably followed.

This is a view not supported by the very different results of a similar incident half a century later. On 22 November 1963 President Kennedy was assassinated by an ex-Communist who had recently returned from residence in the Soviet Union accompanied by his Russian wife. With the President, as always whenever and wherever he moved, was an apparatus of subordinates and communications designed to enable him to order the instant destruction of the Soviet Union, long regarded as the deadly enemy of the United States and as constantly plotting the subversion by every conceivable means of all that Americans held most dear. It was a combination of circumstances perfectly adapted, in the eyes of the determinist, to produce an unwanted but unavoidable war.

What actually happened was revealingly different. As soon as the first garbled agency message reached Washington, the U.S. Secretary of Defence and the Joint Chiefs of Staff alerted all American armed forces throughout the world. They did so before they even knew the President was dead, let alone the identity or the strange career of his assailant. At the moment of this order there was no question of foreign involvement, of culpability, even of an objectionable act. But a factor of instability had been introduced and at once there was a potential crisis. Those concerned had no reason to suppose that an external threat existed – and when the revelation of the assassin's record raised that presumption, they discounted it – but developments had suddenly become unpredictable and they reacted accordingly.

This was perhaps an unusually sensitive response to an incident with no immediately apparent international implications, but the Government of the United States, more than any other, are accustomed to poise tremendous issues on a knife-edge of stability and predictability. And, with their chief decision-taker incapacitated, with his deputy in the danger zone, with half the Cabinet in an aircraft over the Pacific, there must have been an overwhelming impression that the situation was suddenly fluid, that events were escaping from their control and that, in the words of the general order, this was the time 'to be especially on the alert'.[1]

There are three morals in this story. The first is that it is premature to despair of human intelligence. In spite of a concatenation of the most adverse circumstances pessimism could devise, there was neither war nor thought of war. On the contrary, if the incident had any effect on American-Russian relations, it was one of alleviation through mutual relief of tension.

[1] See William Manchester, *Death of a President* (Michael Joseph 1967).

The second moral is that, entirely without regard to the Apparent nature and quality of the event, any sudden and unexpected change is a potential source of crisis if it convinces a government that the immediate future is no longer predictable.

The third moral is that there is a difference between provoking instability and seeking change: it is the difference between a skid and a turn. The former may ultimately prove far less significant, it may constitute only the most momentary intermission in an unaltered course, but, while it lasts, its end is as unpredictable as its onset was unexpected. In all but the coolest and most skilful of drivers the combination of these two factors is liable to induce a dangerous panic.

That is why governments will often accept and adjust themselves to great changes without ever allowing any consequential dispute to assume serious proportions, yet react with intemperate violence when a lesser change creates a condition of instability. Russian development of thermo-nuclear weapons effected a far greater and more lasting change in Soviet-American relations than anything threatened by the mere transfer of a few missiles to Cuba; the independence of India was a transformation that made the nationalization of the Suez Canal Company seem utterly insignificant. But these great changes had been foreseen: there had been time for the driver to realize that he was approaching a bend and must turn his wheel. Admittedly he could still turn it the wrong way, as the Austrians deliberately did in 1914, but the risks of considered error are probably less than those of impulsive reaction. As long as the leaders of nations are human, instability and crisis are most likely to result from those actions which are not merely objectionable, but also involve a change that is sudden, surprising and of unpredictable extent.

The element of change is nevertheless fundamental. Most Israeli attacks on her Arab neighbours during 1968 and 1969 have been sudden and surprising, nor has their intended extent always been immediately predictable. But the bloodless raid against Beirut Airport on 28 December 1968 produced a degree of crisis not attained by crueller and more destructive air-raids on Jordan or artillery duels across the Suez Canal. These were familiar incidents, part of an established pattern. They might shock, but did not surprise. The Beirut raid, however, was sufficiently unexpected to imply a change in the relationship of Israel and the Lebanon and to suggest the existence of disturbingly altered Israeli intentions.

There are thus two distinct causes of crisis: surprise and change. These are not self-sufficient, even in combination. The most astonishing of changes − a Soviet proclamation of unilateral and total disarmament, for instance − would not provoke a crisis if nobody regarded it as an objectionable act. A crisis is only an aggravated dispute and a dispute only arises when objection is manifested by one government to the conduct of another. But, as was earlier argued, the factors that aggravate disputes are often more significant than the actions which initiate them. An objectionable act can only be defined in tautological terms, because the actions which either always arouse objection, or else never do so, are too few to be made the subject of any usefully general rule. Nor is there much practical need for such a definition:

it is not difficult to decide whether the action of another government is disadvantageous and, hence, objectionable. The hard and crucial questions are whether or not to manifest objection and, if so, in what manner.

It is because surprise and change tend to aggravate disputes that they are useful — to both sides — as indicators of their potentially critical nature. Governments committing objectionable acts often persuade themselves that these are so thoroughly in accord with all the most unimpeachable principles of morality that only the most evil of enemies could take exception to them. They might find it easier to admit that there was nevertheless an element of surprising change capable of eliciting an otherwise irrational reaction from a startled statesman. The latter might equally benefit from realizing that the more he was startled, the greater was his need for care in the reaching of decisions. Surprise, moreover, may often be disproportionate to the degree of Real change revealed by later analysis. And it is change that is the more important factor of the two.

In 1939 the instability produced by the Nazi-Soviet Pact owed little to the surprising nature of this event and everything to the real change it effected in international relationships. The effect would scarcely have been inferior if the preliminary negotiations had been as prolonged and as publicized as the abortive Soviet discussions with Britain and France. This agreement, incidentally, is also an instance of the irrelevance of moral arguments as a test of the objectionable character of international actions or of their capacity to cause crises. It was scarcely open to Britain and France to blame Germany for her success in achieving what they had attempted in vain, but the news was nevertheless universally accepted as the harbinger of war. Even the Chamberlain Government took immediate precautionary measures.

Change, however, is a more elusive indicator than surprise. The objectionable act that itself effects a change in international relationships may not be too difficult to identify, but what about those actions that merely reveal an intention to bring about change in the future? The Chinese Government, for instance, have for many years manifested the intention of seeking changes in almost all directions. The consequences have been very various, ranging from the acute crises over Korea in 1950 and Formosa in 1958, to entirely abortive outbursts of empty abuse. Should every manifestation of Chinese intentions have been treated as a crisis-indicator?

Broadly speaking, and making due allowance for the extent to which such manifestations lose their apparent force through conformity to a pattern recognized as that of mere gesture, the answer must be yes. Admittedly the endless reiteration of Chinese belligerence over Vietnam — 'the Chinese people will staunchly side with the Vietnamese people and fight shoulder to shoulder with them to the end'[1] — has induced considerable scepticism concerning the significance of Chinese bluster, but a government with the ability to impose a change in international relationships should be taken seriously in the absence of strong indications to the contrary. After all, we are at present only concerned with the signals that should prompt further analysis. If this is

[1] Command 2756 of 1965, doc. 24 (H.M.S.O.).

needlessly undertaken, only the leisure of the analysts will have been lost, a luxury preserved at undue expense by the Americans in 1950 and by the Indians in the years that preceded 1962.

An evident intention to effect change should always stimulate questions: would it be disadvantageous, is it seriously intended, could it be unilaterally accomplished? It may be that these questions must very often be asked, that the answers will frequently be negative or uncertain, that the effort is greater than the existing resources of governmental intellect and information could conveniently bear. If so, then these resources should be increased. The expense of devoting deep analysis to problems that ultimately prove unimportant is negligible by comparison with the cost of neglecting this precaution in a single grave dispute.

For it must unfortunately be admitted that, although the concepts of instability, of change, of surprise may assist in the discrimination of the Real and the Apparent, they are nevertheless neither infallible nor sufficient indicators of crisis. The more we search for short cuts, the more expedients we explore in our anxiety to avoid increasing the numbers of officials or the burdens of statesmen, the more we are driven, however reluctantly, to the conclusion that there exists no substitute for the thorough analysis of every dispute in the light of the terminal situations that may reasonably be deduced from the respective purposes, resources and intentions of the contestants. If change is a criterion for this process, its value is largely negative: an objectionable act that neither effects nor implies change, that does not startle or threaten instability, is unlikely to provoke a crisis. The exclusion of this category of objectionable acts is scarcely a major achievement.

VI — TERMINAL SITUATIONS

Prolonged argument has thus elicited pointers rather than touchstones. The objectionable act, surprise, instability, the evidence of change or the presumed intention to effect it: these are concepts which may assist in identifying the symptoms of crisis, but they are not the clear-cut, fool-proof indicators we might have hoped to find. As a background, rather than a basis, for decision, they may nevertheless offer certain minor advantages.

The first is that, vague and abstract though they may be, these concepts do provide an approach to a neutral and unemotional language for describing the critical features of international disputes. Because they could be applied by both sides these concepts might thus facilitate the mutual comprehension of purposes and intentions.

The second advantage is that all these pointers tend towards the same conclusion: the overriding importance of terminal situations. The adjective 'terminal' is nowadays commonly applied to the last illnesses of individual human beings, but the progress of technology has made it equally relevant to the race as a whole. When we consider the possible outcome of certain disputes, it is no longer a matter of mere fantasy to include among our hypotheses the extinction of much of the species. And, as long as this remains a conceivable result of disputes, it must surely follow that their end is more important than their beginning.

Nor is it only because of what Raymond Aron has called 'l'extension planétaire du système diplomatique',[1] that this concept ought to be applied to all disputes, even those apparently incapable of involving the ultimate perils of thermo-nuclear conflict. Modern communications, the widespread diffusion of the interests of the Great Powers, their interlocking alliances and their intersecting ideological rivalries have made it more difficult to predict the limits of any dispute, but there are still some where the subject matter or the relationship between the contestants seem to exclude the possibility of extreme or violent repercussions. It is scarcely conceivable that a dispute between Britain and Denmark over fishing rights, or between Britain and New Zealand over the price of butter, could ever lead to any of the more dramatic consequences on which attention has hitherto been focused. Nevertheless such disputes are more likely to reach an advantageous solution if the decisions taken on both sides are guided by an assessment of terminal situations. If a Danish fishery protection vessel fires a shot across the bows of a British trawler, no amount of excited talk about the High Seas is likely to lead to war, but it could easily impair Anglo-Danish relations and curb the mutually profitable growth of Anglo-Danish trade.

No dispute is intrinsically too trivial or, in its Apparent aspects, too one-sided or predestined, to deserve less than rational consideration, nor can reason demand less of those who take decisions than to consider their actions in the light of their probable consequences. It is a hard

[1] Raymond Aron, *Peace and War: A Theory of International Relations,* Chapter 15 (Weidenfeld & Nicolson 1966).

requirement always to ask, before beginning a dispute, how it may be expected to end, but this examination has revealed no alternative. The Reality of any dispute is most nearly capable of apprehension through a comparison of the various terminal situations to which different courses of action might reasonably be expected to lead. That this process should depend on prediction, to which we must now turn our attention, rather than on intuition, is no disadvantage, for prediction, however difficult and fallible, is the scientific method of assembling awkward facts into a coherent and comprehensible system, whereas intuition is the gambler's judgement that Reality resides in a particular aspect of its diverse Appearances.

3

PREDICTION

'This is the second time in our history that there has come
back from Germany to Downing Street peace with honour.
I believe it is peace for our time.'

Neville Chamberlain[1]

PREDICTION is a necessary preliminary to
rational decision, for any action taken without regard
to its consequences emanates from mental processes
undisciplined by reason: emotion issues in impulse or
instinct triggers a reflex. But decision implies a choice
between at least two possible courses of action: the minimum options open are to do something or to do nothing.
To exert a useful influence on decision, a prediction
must permit discrimination by indicating the likely
results of each choice in terms sufficiently specific to
allow its advantages to be compared with those of others.
It must also be finite, so as to suggest the incidence,
both in time and space, of the predicted consequences.
'The wages of sin are death' may indicate a disincentive;
it may even be true; but it does not specify whose death
or even roughly when this might occur. As, in the long
run, we shall all be dead, sinners and saints alike, this is
not a helpful prediction.

[1] Speech of 30 September 1938 on his return from the Munich
Conference – quoted in Feiling, *Life of Neville Chamberlain* (Macmillan
1946).

On the other hand, the prophecy that the world would end in A.D. 1000 did have one useful feature: it was verifiable. On 1 January 1001 all those concerned were able to note that the inaccuracy of this prediction had been satisfactorily demonstrated and thus to conclude that similar arguments from similar premises could safely be taken less seriously on future occasions. Whenever a prediction can be proved or disproved, this creates at least a chance of increasing the accuracy of the next prediction.

A useful prediction is thus one which suggests answers to three questions:

will the result be good or bad?

who will do what and when?

will the result really occur?

The last question can only be answered with any approach to certainty after the event, but, unless it can be answered then, no antecedent guess is possible, nor is any subsequent analysis of the validity of the arguments employed.

These requirements are seldom met by political predictions, least of all those concerned with international affairs. Politicians are human. They know that the behaviour of other human beings can not be predicted with certainty and that a high proportion of mistaken prophecies is inevitable. Rather than risk the exposure of their own fallibility by making specific predictions, they seek refuge from error in ambiguity, a tradition old before Delphi was built. Instead of saying that the action taken by the British Government will cause this or that other government to make some specific move, the politician prefers to forecast the consequences of British action in abstract or metaphorical terms. These usually suggest that the result will somehow be advantageous, but not who will do what or when. It is thus difficult, even after the event, to attribute error to the orator, but equally hard to be sure whether the prediction was right or wrong or to derive any useful lesson from the outcome. With a series of similar predictions, the visible results of each should constitute a touchstone for the accuracy of the next, but, if the first was ambiguous, the last will still be a leap in the dark.

It would, of course, be both unfair and misleading to regard the preservation of ambiguity as the sole motive for the politician's habit of Delphic utterance. When policy has to be justified before large audiences, it would often be imprudent to explain that the decision of the British Government was intended to induce a particular foreign government to take some specific action. It is easier and more acceptable to say that it will bring 'peace' or 'honour' or 'stability'. Unfortunately, what begins as a public convenience soon becomes a private vice: metaphors and abstractions invade the inmost recesses of Downing Street and Whitehall: concrete actions are taken by the British Government in pursuit of objectives of a nebulous and metaphysical character. The classical example is Lord Avon's telegram to President Eisenhower on 27 July 1956:

> 'My colleagues and I are convinced that we must be ready, in the last resort, to use force to bring Nasser to his senses. For our part we are prepared to do so. I have this morning instructed our Chiefs of Staff to prepare a military plan accordingly.'[1]

It will be interesting, in due course, to read the

[1] Anthony Eden, *Full Circle* (op. cit.).

'Intention' paragraph of that military plan, but the evidence so far published suggests that there never was a specific prediction that, once military operations had reached a certain stage, President Nasser would either himself take a defined step of an advantageous character or else be replaced by a named person who would do so. The whole prediction was that 'force' would bring Nasser 'to his senses': how, when or in what manner were not indicated. This was not, of course, the first occasion on which a British Government made the assumption that their opponent was a lunatic who could be cured, as it was thought King George III had been, by the use of violence. But it admirably illustrates the applicability to political prediction of Fowler's guide to the correct writing of English:

'prefer the concrete word to the abstract'[1]

Nevertheless, there are limits to the ability of even the ideal Foreign Secretary to support his proposals by predicting their results in the rigorously concrete terms so far suggested. These limits are not necessarily set by the human fallibility of the predictor – it is still better for him to be wrong than vague – but by the sheer complexity of his data. The immediate results of any concrete action can usually be predicted in concrete and specific terms, often with a fair degree of accuracy. According to Hugh Thomas, the Joint Planning Staff of the Ministry of Defence did this so efficiently over Suez that their report had to be suppressed.[2] It is the secondary, indirect, remoter, later, more lasting repercussions that

[1] H. W. & F. G. Fowler, *The King's English*, Chapter I (Oxford University Press 1930).

[2] Hugh Thomas, *The Suez Affair*, Epilogue (Weidenfeld & Nicolson 1966).

are so hard to envisage in concrete terms. Any important move by a major power is a heavy stone dropped into a pool full of startled frogs: there is no telling when or where the last of the intersecting ripples will reach the shore or what sensitive plants it will there disturb.

As these words are written,[1] there are 125 members of the United Nations. By the time these words are read, there will probably be more than 125 and both totals will exclude several important countries. All these 125 odd governments are capable of some reaction to any important move by the British Government. Let us imagine a Foreign Secretary faced with a decision of this kind. He has already devoted considerable time and thought to hammering out the ideal primary prediction. He is then asked about the secondary effects. How can he even find the hours — for important decisions have an awkward tendency to be at once urgent and controversial, hence time-consuming — to guess what each of these governments will do, not immediately, but when they have had time to think about it, to consult one another, to observe the first results, to make up their minds? Even the chess champion playing a dozen opponents simultaneously does not have to consider combinations and permutations on this scale — and chess at least has rigid rules.

It is conceivable that, in some distant future, some fantastic computer will come up with 125 predictions, weight them, analyse them and deliver a compound, vectored verdict. At present this is not a practical proposition. There are limits, though it would be hard to define them, to the possibilities of precise prediction.

[1] October 1968.

As a working argument it may be suggested that the immediate consequences of any rational action should always be capable of description in concrete and specific terms. Beyond the point of first reactions the process of secondary prediction must be curtailed if it is to be attempted at all. Only approximations can be regarded as practical.

Broadly speaking there seem to be four customary approaches to secondary prediction in the field of international affairs. The first is to assume that only the immediate consequences matter and that these will dictate the general character of the secondary repercussions. The second is to identify a few governments as those whose reactions will matter and to concentrate on predicting them. The third is to regard secondary repercussions as determined by the intrinsic nature of the action and to rely on precedent for their prediction. The fourth is to assume the existence of something called world opinion and to predict its reactions on the basis of the ethical content of the move in question. All these approaches will be considered in the following analysis, but this will concentrate on the fourth, because it is prediction of the effects on world opinion that relies most heavily on abstract and metaphorical language and thus runs counter to the arguments earlier outlined on primary predictions.

Moreover, there is a case here for the abstract which did not exist before. As long as it was possible to predict results in concrete terms, this was obviously preferable. But, if the question 'who will do what and when?' has to be projected over so many countries or so far ahead that, for practical purposes, it becomes unanswerable in detail, then a degree of generalization becomes inevitable and there may be greater attractions in forecasting results in terms of the 'honour', 'prestige' or 'good name' of Britain, provided these and similar terms can be shown to constitute approximations with a useful significance to match their emotional content.

That they possess an emotional content is not in itself reprehensible. It is the common experience of everyday life that emotive words are regularly used as a convenient shorthand for justifying decisions with solid roots in material advantage. A banker may say that it would be 'dishonest' to repudiate the unwitnessed oral promise he subsequently regrets: it would take him longer to explain why this might ultimately lose him even more money than keeping his word. But he could do so: he could argue that it is the custom of the City of London for very large sums to change hands on the strength of a moment's conversation, that this is only possible among people who trust one another completely and that failure to honour an unprofitable undertaking would result in exclusion from the charmed circle and the loss of future business. This would be a rational explanation of the way in which an immediate and particular advantage could subsequently be outweighed by adverse repercussions of a more general character. In this context, therefore, the concept of 'honesty' is a convenient touchstone for a busy banker: it enables him to reach immediate decisions on practical problems by asking himself a single, simple question.

But the qualification 'in this context' is all-important. Absolute integrity may govern all the banker's dealings with his peers in the City of London: it does not follow that the same principle will apply in his relations with his wife. Nor will he expect from non-bankers, or in transactions of a different character, that the concept of integrity will offer a reliable guide to decisions or their consequences. The banker's honesty is a conventional method of pursuing his commercial advantage: it is not an absolute and universally applicable moral standard. It is a useful piece of shorthand because it helps to predict the ultimate results of a particular kind of decision.

It would obviously be convenient to dispose of similar tools in foreign policy. When a Foreign Secretary considers a proposal for action, it is not always enough for him to inquire what are the predicted effects on the particular problem it is intended to solve. Even in some trivial dispute over fishing rights one government may be as much concerned with creating a 'precedent' as with catching pilchards; the other may care less about fishermen than about 'face'. Each is trying to employ these slogans as contractions of far more complex arguments concerning the ultimate effect on wider interests of particular decisions. Are these, and similar words, capable of becoming, in the vast arena of international affairs, useful links in a chain of reasoning as valid as that which supported the banker's honesty in the close and charmed circle of the City of London?

Many people seem to hold this view. For instance, during the latter half of 1968 the British Press were much exercised by the arrival of Soviet troops in Czechoslovakia and numerous attempts were made to predict the ultimate consequences, not in Czechoslovakia itself, but as repercussions on Soviet relations with other governments and on other problems with which the Soviet Government were or might become concerned. Most of these predictions were made in abstract terms and the following is a typical example taken from *The Economist* of 24 August 1968:

> 'an enterprise which is bound to have a calamitous effect on Russia's standing in the world at large and in the communist movement.'

This is obviously not a concrete prediction. It makes no attempt to answer the question 'who will do what and when?' But, if the prediction had been 'a calamitous effect on Russia's credit-worthiness in the London loan market', the abstract terminology would have pointed to a concrete result: the Soviet Union would have found it more difficult to borrow money in London. 'Standing', however, is a vaguer word than 'credit-worthiness' and 'the world at large' a much less restricted context. Even the apparently distinctive phrase 'the communist movement' inevitably provokes the question 'which one?' On the face of it, and bearing in mind the rigorous criteria earlier suggested, this scarcely seems a useful prediction.

Yet it is an attempt to answer a real and necessary question. When the proposal to send troops into Czechoslovakia was being considered in the Kremlin and those concerned had satisfied themselves about the immediate results to be expected, someone must have inquired about the likelihood of side-effects, of wider, more lasting, less direct and concrete repercussions. We know such issues were at least raised in the British

Cabinet before the first bombers headed for Egypt in 1956.[1]

To establish the necessity and importance of such questions it is enough to recall the remarkable differences between the primary and the secondary consequences of earlier interventions in Czechoslovakia. In 1938, for instance, a series of German threats induced the British and French governments to bully Czechoslovakia into ceding the Sudetenland to Germany. Both the British and German governments could regard the primary results with qualified satisfaction: one had avoided a war; the other had acquired part of Czechoslovakia. But the secondary repercussions were altogether different. At home Chamberlain had aroused the bitter opposition and distrust of a minority that was eventually to prove more influential than the masses who accorded him an uncritical adulation; abroad he had given the impression of being not merely ready, but eager, to yield to threats. Hitler, on the other hand, had disarmed his highly placed internal opponents and convinced many of his external foes that compromise was not only preferable to resistance, but the only alternative to defeat. The immediate results of the Munich agreement, curiously enough, seem to have pleased Chamberlain more than they did Hitler, but, until the next German move, the wider and later repercussions were wholly to Germany's advantage.

In 1939 German occupation of the rest of Czechoslovakia seemed to bring immediate gain to Germany and little concrete loss to Britain, where Chamberlain's cool comment was that this had released the British

[1] Hugh Thomas, op. cit.

Government from any obligation to Czechoslovakia. But the secondary repercussions were astonishingly different. In Britain Chamberlain was driven to offer his desperate guarantee to Poland and hence to precipitate the Second World War. In Germany Hitler was confirmed in his view that Britain would always give way and that he could safely disregard the utterances of her exasperated but effete rulers. The occupation of Prague seemed to Hitler 'the greatest day of my life' and, when he added that 'I shall go down to history as the greatest German',[1] he was surely expecting subsequent repercussions to be no less advantageous. Yet, in the hindsight of history, this day of easy victory is seen as the beginning of the end for the Thousand Year Reich and, incidentally, for the British Empire as well.

We know much less about the expectations of the Soviet Government when, in 1948, they encouraged and perhaps assisted the Czech Communist Party to complete the transformation of Czechoslovakia into a People's Republic. Indeed, it is still too early for a precise assessment of the secondary repercussions of this smooth and immediately successful operation. But it is at least arguable that it was partly responsible for a number of decisions by what subsequently came to be called the Western Powers, that these decisions damaged Soviet interests and that they might not have been taken, at least so soon and so whole-heartedly, if the Czech coup had not occurred.[2] The Brussels Treaty, the North Atlantic Treaty, the revision of Western policy towards

[1] Alan Bullock, *Hitler* (Odhams Press 1964).
[2] See, for instance, Chapter 17 of *Memoirs* by George F. Kennan (Hutchinson 1968).

Germany, the decision to defend West Berlin and most of the more concrete manifestations of the Cold War all followed the events in Czechoslovakia, which were frequently invoked by Western statesmen justifying these new policies. In so far as intervention in Czechoslovakia was a real contributory cause of Western efforts to organize an effective and united opposition to the Soviet Union, it is unlikely that this was intended or even foreseen by Stalin. It would be going too far to say that greater foresight would necessarily have resulted in a different Soviet decision, but their simultaneous readiness to tolerate the exclusion of the Communists from the Government of Finland suggests that other options were at least conceivable.

Here then, in a single country and a single decade, were three interventions of which the secondary repercussions bore little relation either to the primary results or to one another. In 1939, at least, the secondary repercussions were also far more important to all concerned – except perhaps to the people of Czechoslovakia. It is thus natural that, in 1968, a fourth intervention should stimulate attempts to predict its ultimate consequences. Indeed, when someone talks of 'a calamitous effect on Russia's standing', he presumably means that, whereas Czechoslovakia and the opponents of intervention in that country could be expected to offer no initial resistance, this Russian move would ultimately cause someone to do something seriously disadvantageous to the Soviet Union. Should this have been predicted in the Kremlin and how do governments set about predicting the ultimate consequences of actions which they expect to be immediately advantageous?

One method has already emerged, even from a sketchy analysis of earlier interventions, as unreliable: in two cases out of three initial reactions did not set the pattern for future repercussions. Nor does the record suggest that it was safe to assume that other governments would do what they had done last time and go on doing it. Western reactions to the Communization of Czechoslovakia were very different to those which had followed similar, and sometimes more violent, measures in Bulgaria, Hungary, Poland and Rumania. And, if precedent were a sufficient basis for prediction, Hitler could scarcely be blamed for expecting his challenge to the British guarantee to Poland to produce little more than the bluster and bluff that had followed the solemn British warning about Czechoslovakia in May 1938 and their affirmation on 4 October 1938 of a 'moral obligation' to guarantee the new frontiers of that country. Nor would such a calculation have constituted a blind or slavish reliance on precedent as the sole guide. On any rational appraisal of British interests a war which had not been worth fighting in September 1938 or March 1939 was still less so in September 1939. Similarly, why should the Western Powers, having manifested their practical indifference to the fate of Czechoslovakia in 1938 and 1939 and having deliberately allowed Russian armies to occupy that country in 1945, suddenly react in 1948 to what the Soviet Government might well have considered the natural and predictable consequence of their earlier actions?

This is not to argue that precedents are unimportant. On the contrary, the most significant result of Russian repression of the Hungarian revolution of 1956 was

what the dog did *not* do in the night: there was no
American military reaction. This precedent must have
played an important part in the Kremlin's deliberations
before 20 August 1968. But precedent alone is an
inadequate guide. Every important action creates a new
situation in which even a close approximation to repe-
tition of the previous action is likely to have different
effects. Moreover this situation exists as much in the
minds of governments as it does in the seemingly more
concrete and objective facts. If one disregards the mental
processes of the British Government, then Hitler's
military and diplomatic chances of getting his way without serious opposition had steadily improved from May
1938, when even he was taken aback by the vigour of
British and French representations, through September
1938, when his generals were sufficiently appalled by
the danger to plot against him, to September 1939, by
which time he had eliminated Czechoslovakia and
Russia as potential enemies, won over his internal
opponents, consolidated his Western defences and
established a tradition of British acceptance of his *faits
accomplis* which the French would be only too happy to
follow. Indeed, when one considers how nearly Germany
won the war in 1940, one realizes how desperate a
gamble was the British ultimatum of 3 September 1939
and one altogether fails to understand those historians
who treat Hitler as a lunatic and Chamberlain as a
rational, if mistaken, man. If Hitler is to be blamed, it
must surely be because he took too practical and short-
sighted a view and made insufficient allowance for the
disturbing effects of emotion on his supposedly phleg-
matic opponents.

Above all, what Hitler had failed to observe was that, although the immediate and concrete reaction of the British Government had been even more futile and pusillanimous in March 1939 than in September 1938 (when they had at least mobilized the Fleet), the March intervention had nevertheless started a fundamental and adverse transformation in the climate of opinion, the basic preconceptions and the emotional attitudes of the British Government and of some of their supporters. As a result, they were ready, against all rational expectation, not only to declare war, but to reject the peace offer made after the elimination of Poland and to continue the fight after their shattering defeat in 1940.

How is this irrational British behaviour to be explained and how could it have been predicted?

Some British historians prefer a moral answer. Their argument is that German expansion up to and including the acquisition of the Sudetenland in 1938 could all be justified by the principle of nationality: the German Government were only re-incorporating Germans arbitrarily excluded from membership of the German nation. In March 1939, however, Hitler extended his rule to non-German peoples and he also broke his word to Chamberlain.[1] He thus committed two immoral actions which, for the first time, convinced the British people that his intentions were evil and dangerous, thus enabling the British Government to count on popular support for

[1] This argument was employed by the British Foreign Secretary in his speech to the House of Lords on 20 March 1939, but its moral force was perhaps impaired by its phrasing: 'Herr Hitler appealed to the principle of self-determination . . . on which the British Empire itself has been erected' — a remarkable sentiment from a former Viceroy of India. Command 6106 of 1939.

war. If accepted, such an explanation might then offer other governments a basis for predicting the secondary reactions of the British Government: will the British people be morally outraged?

The attraction of this moral explanation of the events of 1939 is that it appears to offer an answer to the really difficult question. This is not, contrary to popular belief, why was appeasement pursued so long, but why was it so rashly and precipitately abandoned? What is really bewildering is why Chamberlain, conscious that British rearmament was incomplete, profoundly sceptical of Russian assistance, aware that Poland could neither defend herself nor be helped by Britain, should have reversed his first reaction to the occupation of Prague

'I am not prepared to engage this country by new un-specified commitments, operating under conditions which can not now be foreseen.'[1]

and issued his extraordinary guarantee to Poland. It would be a neat hypothesis to assume that a sudden wave of moral indignation overcame the prudence of the government and the fears of the people.

There is a simpler if less creditable explanation. The occupation of Prague frightened both government and people out of their wits.

As Churchill subsequently put it, when deploring Chamberlain's decision 'to fight with all the odds against you'

'there may even be a worse case. You may have to fight when there is no hope of victory, because it is better to perish than live as slaves.'[2]

[1] Keith Feiling, *Life of Neville Chamberlain*, Chapter 26.
[2] W. S. Churchill, *The Gathering Storm*, op. cit.

It was this last fear that Hitler had aroused by occupying Prague in such swift defiance of the Munich Agreement, the fear that German expansion had acquired so accelerating a momentum that Britain must force a fight before all her potential allies were engulfed and she was left to defend herself alone.

In practice, of course, this was just what she had to do and, in retrospect, it seems that a further postponement of the war might have offered Britain more gain than loss. But, when fear overcomes reason, a period of paralysis is often followed by a desperate spurt of inappropriate activity and, whichever explanation we prefer of British conduct in 1939, this must necessarily be of an irrational character. Needless to say, it was the decision that was irrational, not the fear that prompted it. It was not unreasonable, if over-optimistic, to regard March 1939 as the point at which the realization of Hitler's ambitions became a more frightening prospect than a war: the mistake lay in not choosing a more advantageous moment for fighting it. But no ethical theory capable of commanding the credence, or influencing the decisions, of foreigners has yet been advanced to explain why the Munich Agreement was peace with honour and the 1939 declaration of war a moral necessity. It does not matter how many Englishmen sincerely held such views at the time: foreigners could not be expected to believe either in their sincerity or in their readiness to fight for so strange a hypothesis. As explained elsewhere,[1] this is the general weakness of moral arguments in international affairs: they do not travel well. Hope and fear, however, are universal and more easily predictable.

[1] See Grant Hugo, op. cit.

This analysis does suggest one method which Hitler might have employed to reach a more accurate prediction of the secondary consequences of his intervention in March 1939. This was to concentrate on assessing the relative incidence of hope and fear, and the extent to which these emotions might be expressed in action, which his moves had aroused in his principal opponent. In 1939 this was undoubtedly the British Government. Nobody else, not even potentially more important enemies such as Russia and the United States, was going to *do* anything without a British initiative and perhaps not even then. This was not an easy task, and as we know, Hitler was in any case willing to risk a war he expected to win. But it does suggest a lesson for more cautious governments anxious to eat their cake without fighting for it.

Even when narrowed down to one or more key governments and to the critical reactions of hope and fear, the question 'who will do what and when?' still presents a more difficult problem to the predictor than vaguer formulations of an abstract and ethical character. But, however hard it may be to arrive at an accurate answer, this will be more useful. The avoidance of ambiguity is more important than the apparent avoidance of error.

This emerges clearly from the seeming vindication by events of the prediction earlier quoted from *The Economist* of 24 August 1968: 'a calamitous effect on Russia's standing in the world at large.'

A month later, on 26 September, the Secretary-General of the United Nations, perhaps the most plausible contemporary claimant to infallibility in the

proclamation of doctrine concerning international faith
and morals, noted in his annual report to the General
Assembly:

> 'a serious decline in the standards of international ethics and
> morality'

and

> 'deplored the action of the Soviet Union and four of its Warsaw
> Pact allies in sending their armed forces into Czechoslovakia
> in late August 1968.'[1]

We need waste no time arguing about the motives of
the governments which endorsed (and had, in many cases,
anticipated) U Thant's disapproval, but which did not
accept his report's corresponding references to intervention in Vietnam or the Dominican Republic. It would
be naïve to suppose that their attitude – or that of the
governments who either supported Russian intervention
or else wondered what all the fuss was about – was
determined solely by the nature and quality of the act
under discussion. For practical purposes it may be conceded that, in so far as Russia's standing in the world at
large depends on speeches in the United Nations and
similar expressions of opinion, this had deteriorated
since 20 August 1968. The enemies of the Soviet
Union now had a new propaganda argument at their
disposal.

This was one secondary repercussion of Soviet intervention which, in so far as it was implicit in *The
Economist*'s prediction, undoubtedly occurred. But both
the prediction and the consequences extended further.

[1] Quoted in *The Times*, 27 September 1968.

The first said 'calamitous'; the second was explained in U Thant's report:

> 'The repercussions of this act of sheer military power were felt around the world and have engendered a feeling of dismay, uneasiness and insecurity.'

Once again we need not quibble over 'around the world'. Not all governments shared the Secretary-General's sentiments and, for those who did, emotional intensity varied inversely to the distance separating their frontiers from those of the Soviet Union. These are details. Broadly speaking, we may agree that this move aroused fear and that this fear, if neither universal nor uniform, was at least as widespread as its function: moral disapproval.

This, however, gives us two results of different kinds: disapproval and fear. The first can seldom if ever be regarded as advantageous to the government incurring it, whereas most governments occasionally, and some governments usually, consider it both useful and desirable to inspire fear. Although apparently correct this prediction thus fails our first test: its answer to the question – will the result be good or bad? – is ambiguous. Indeed, when considered from the Soviet standpoint – the right one if the function of predictions is to influence decisions – the answer may actually be wrong. What would have been the reaction of the Soviet leaders if, in mid-August, they had not merely had foreknowledge of the Secretary-General's words, but had accepted as an accurate description of the repercussions of the decision then contemplated: 'dismay, uneasiness and insecurity'? They would surely have said that these were neither inappropriate nor unwelcome reactions to the exercise of Soviet power. The violent and ignominious death of the Caesar Caligula has never lessened the attraction to governments, irrespective of nationality or ideology, of his maxim: *'oderint dum metuant'*. Great Powers, in particular, soon become inured to the disapproval which is almost a function of their status: they do not inquire whether others will praise or blame, but what they will *do*. Stalin's question — 'how many divisions has the Pope?' — would surely have been applied by his successors to the Secretary-General of the United Nations. They might even have added that 'Russia's standing in the world at large' would be positively enhanced by the alarm they had aroused and that this would facilitate the attainment of their objectives elsewhere.

Such an answer might have been supported by precedent — an unreliable argument but one dear to all governments. Their Hungarian intervention of 1956 had inspired the same Western predictions of calamitous effects; had received similar condemnation in the United Nations; had also thinned the ranks and diluted the allegiance of Western Communist Parties. But what did anyone *do*? How did Soviet interests suffer? What concrete manifestations of foreign disapproval had left any trace ten years later? How much even survived the launching of the first Russian Sputnik in 1957?

Such predictions, of course, would have been no more useful than any others based on 'standing' or similar abstract generalizations. What secondary predictions ought to have been made in the Kremlin and how might these have been reached?

To answer this question certain assumptions are

necessary. These are not based on evidence — too little is known of the nature of deliberations behind those astounding walls — but on theory.[1]

The first of these assumptions is that the Soviet leaders regarded the authority and social order of their nation-state as menaced by any continuation, let alone extension, of the reform movement in Czechoslovakia and that this interpretation of their national interest was reinforced by national aspirations of an ideological character. The second is that they expected their troops to eliminate this threat without interference from the United States or any other country.

If they had gone on from these primary predictions to consider secondary repercussions, they might have begun with the Soviet Union's various client governments: the actual satellites, the autonomous Communist régimes and the non-Communist governments dependent on Soviet favour either because of geographical proximity or as recipients of important Soviet assistance. This prediction can have presented few problems: loyal governments would be encouraged by this evidence of their protector's strength and determination; disloyal neighbours would be frightened into watching their step.[2] Distant governments, admittedly, would have a theoretical option. Not being themselves exposed to

[1] For this theory and a definition and analysis of the terms used in the following paragraph, see Grant Hugo, op. cit.

[2] Since these words were first written, Yugoslavia has been suggested as an exception, so the following quotation from *The Times* of 23 October 1969 may be of interest: 'Mr. Zoran Gluscevic, former editor of the fortnightly publication *Knjizevne Novine*, is to be put on trial next Tuesday for writing an article on the Soviet occupation of Czechoslovakia in which he condemned the behaviour of Soviet troops in order to warn Yugoslavs of the danger to their country.'

immediate Soviet intervention, they might have profited by this lesson to seek a less dangerous protector before the growth of the Soviet Navy brought them within the ambit of Soviet discipline. But, when one considers actual cases – Cuba, Egypt, North Vietnam, Syria – where else could they turn? The effect on client governments would thus be beneficial, whether by fortifying hope or by arousing salutary fear.

Hostile governments would naturally be the next subject for prediction. Many of them had previously reacted to the arousal of fear, not by submission, but by increased preparations for self-defence. Might they not again respond similarly, thus eventually producing a military balance less advantageous to the Soviet Union than any likely to have existed without Soviet intervention in Czechoslovakia? A Soviet predictor would have had to regard this as a possibility, but he might well have considered it unlikely. He would expect the Western Powers, all anxious to reduce their existing military effort, to regard Soviet intervention as a defensive measure, a police operation, a reassertion of one aspect of the *status quo* which the Western Alliance itself existed to preserve. In the unstable Europe of 1948 even a discreet intervention in Czechoslovakia had been seen as a threat demanding urgent defensive preparations lest it be repeated in France or Italy. Now there was no need for alarm: the Soviet Empire was not being extended; its crumbling walls were being shored up. Neither fear, nor interest (a Czechoslovakia held down by Soviet troops was safer for the West than a country liable to erupt into rebellion and cause unpredictable complications); nor ideology (what American would

want to defend one kind of Communism against another?)
would spur the Western powers to the kind of practical
response that might be damaging to Soviet interests, but
would be even more unpopular with Western voters.
The most that hostile governments would do, even in
the long run, would thus be to exploit Soviet intervention for propaganda purposes, a result that would be
disagreeable but tolerable.

Uncommitted governments would command little
attention; being mostly outside Europe they could be
expected to view this local incident with considerable
detachment.

The real difficulty arises only in imagining what might
have been predicted of the reactions of Communist
parties, fellow-travellers and useful revolutionary movements outside the Soviet orbit. The obstacle here is not
one of principle. There are three obvious categories:
ruling parties, tolerated oppositions and persecuted
oppositions. The ruling parties are actuated mainly by
fear: whether of the United States or of their own people
or of the Soviet Union. This preoccupation leaves them
little time for romantic notions and the same is usually
true of persecuted oppositions. They have an immediate
enemy and, as long as they can expect some aid and
succour from the Soviet Union, they are unlikely to
spend much time worrying whether, in the long run,
their distant protector might prove more dangerous than
their actual oppressor. But a tolerated opposition,
whether Communist or fellow-travelling, is not in acute
and immediate fear. Its members are primarily actuated
by hope: that one day, thanks in part to the assistance
and example of the Soviet Union, they will achieve

personal power. It thus matters to them if some Soviet action not only constitutes a public reminder that their eventual power would have to be subordinated to Russian national interests, but also obstructs their path to power by frightening off the more numerous, and politically more naïve, allies on which tolerated oppositions mostly depend. On tactical grounds, therefore, tolerated oppositions had an additional incentive for dissociating themselves from a decision which inspired stimulating rather than salutary fear.

What is puzzling is that so little effort seems to have been made by the Soviet leaders to counteract this one predictably adverse secondary repercussion of their intervention. In the case of Hungary, for instance, there was much less reaction of this kind, in spite of the emotions aroused by the manner in which Hungarians fought and died. This was because care had been taken to set up a pro-Russian government of Hungarian Communists at an early stage and to present a case which foreign Communists and their sympathizers would at least be able to convince themselves was plausible. Moreover, Russian military action on that occasion was immediate, swift and decisive. From start to finish it only lasted a couple of months. It was all over before there was time for most foreign Communists to gear themselves to the unfamiliar processes of independent thought.

This time, however, months of blatant indecision were followed by fumbling and half-hearted action unaccompanied by any adequate political preparation. Suez, rather than Hungary, appeared to have been the model. Whereas foreign governments, conscious of their own fallibility in these matters, were impressed by the immediate results, tolerated oppositions were dismayed by the absence of the stage-management to which they had become accustomed. There were many defections, not merely by individuals, but by actual parties. The extent of the damage is revealed (indeed exaggerated – another sign of inadequate preparation) by the pathetically thin list of foreign Communist endorsements set out under the heading 'The Peoples Will Not Be Hoodwinked' in *On Events in Czechoslovakia*.[1] As these words are written the actual score seems to be: *for* the Soviet Union – 20 persecuted, 8 ruling and 3 tolerated parties; *against* the Soviet Union – 21 tolerated, 4 ruling[2] and 4 persecuted parties.[3]

There are three possible explanations: a failure of prediction (though this might have been that early adverse reactions would soon evaporate once local success had manifestly been achieved); a failure of decision (this may have been deferred too long to permit of political preparation); or a radically different assessment in Moscow of the value of tolerated oppositions.

Whatever actually happened, our ideal predictor should have told the assembled dignitaries in the Kremlin that, provided the immediate objective was achieved in Czechoslovakia without extending military operations outside that country, then the secondary repercussions would be that client governments would pay more heed to Soviet representations; that hostile governments would confine their reactions to words

[1] Published in Moscow by 'A Press Group of Soviet Journalists'.
[2] Two of these – China and Albania – are really 'hostile governments'.
[3] Two of these are anti-Russian anyway.

and innocuous gestures and that only tolerated oppositions would, at least temporarily, reduce the effectiveness
of Soviet efforts at propaganda and subversion by a
display of independence and disapproval. If he added a
recommendation, it might have been that the restoration
of 'normality' in Czechoslovakia should be followed as
soon as possible by a spectacular exploit in space calculated to efface any ill effects that might remain six
months or a year later.

That is the prediction. *Qui vivra verra.*

4

ABSTRACTIONS AND THEIR
APPLICATION

'Ce mot me fut nouveau et inconnu. Jusques-là, j'avois
entendu les affaires, mais ce terme me jetta dans l'obscurité,
et je croy qu'il n'a esté inventé que pour broüiller.'

Pascal[1]

A CERTAIN impatience with the abstract will
scarcely have escaped the attentive reader and may
even have struck him as incongruous in an avowedly
theoretical treatise. If the concrete word is always to be
preferred to the abstract, Reality to Appearance and
prediction to aspiration, what remains to oppose to the
preference of practical men for deciding each issue on its
merits, as it arises, and in the light of judgement formed
primarily by personal experience?

One answer, of course, is that practical men do
nothing of the sort. The 'merits' of an issue are not
objectively existing and intrinsic characteristics: they
are those Apparent features which the preconceptions
of the observer cause him to regard as the most important. And these features, as is evident from the utterances
already quoted of practical men, nearly always take the
form of abstractions. Sir E. Goschen relied on 'honour';
Mr. McNamara justified the war in Vietnam by reference

[1] Blaise Pascal, *Les Provinciales* (Manchester University Press 1919).

to a 'principle'; Senator Robert Kennedy was primarily concerned with the 'moral position of the United States': even *The Economist*, that last refuge of the pragmatist, invested their all in the 'standing' of the Soviet Union.

As earlier suggested, practical men employ these arguments because of their convenience: they are symbols intended to signify readily comprehensible contractions of processes of reasoning it would be tedious and superfluous to elaborate. Anyone who has studied the great work of which the title has been so impertinently borrowed for the present effusion will readily grasp the need for such contractions. In his dissection of Appearance and Reality Bradley remorselessly exposes the meaninglessness of almost everything and his iconoclasm pales before the efforts of some of his successors. If every decision had to be logically derived from unassailable premises, no decision would ever be taken. Whether this would necessarily be a bad thing is debatable but irrelevant: governments exist to take decisions and, as procrastination is a decision in effect if not in intent, will continue to do so. To save time – and thought – these decisions will also be justified, and sometimes prompted, by resort to abstractions.

The practical question – and theorizing on international affairs can never claim greater merit than practical utility – is thus whether some abstractions are more useful than others. The answer is that an abstraction is useful when it describes a concrete situation – whether actual or potential – in terms that facilitate verifiable predictions. The value of this description will be enhanced if it is sufficiently objective to be used by more than one party to the dispute. When the arrival of

Russian nuclear missiles in Cuba was described as objectionable, surprising and productive of instability in Soviet-American relations, all these epithets were abstract and depended for their validity on certain preconceptions of the relationship then existing between the Soviet Union and the United States. But it would have been sheer casuistry for any well-informed, intelligent and rational analyst in the Kremlin to have argued in advance that this action was unlikely to arouse American objections, that it would occasion no surprise and that it need introduce no element of instability. On the other hand, such an analyst would have experienced no difficulty whatever in rejecting the applicability of most of the descriptions actually employed by President Kennedy. He could sincerely — for what sincerity is worth, which is not much — have maintained that this was a purely defensive response to the menace of an American invasion of Cuba, a response in no way different in kind from the installation of American missiles in countries adjacent to the Soviet Union and supposedly threatened by Russian aggression.

In this dispute — and in most others — there are at least three possible sets of abstract descriptions, all of them arguable, even plausible. But one set can be accepted by both sides as at least a half truth, whereas the remainder are wholly acceptable to one and monstrous falsehoods to the other. Therefore, if we are concerned to predict a terminal situation which is not merely desirable, but also likely, any concept wholly repugnant to the other side is unlikely to form the basis of their predictions and hence to offer any useful clue to their intentions. Yet acceptance of the other side's concept as a basis for one's own predictions may not only be humanly difficult, but also inconsistent with one's own purposes. It is scarcely conceivable that, in October 1962, the United States Government could have based any decision on the assumption that Soviet intentions were as essentially defensive, pacific and virtuous as Khruschev subsequently claimed they were. If this crisis ultimately reached a peaceful and, so far, a stable solution, it was only because the two governments involved were able to base their predictions on the assumption that the opponent was neither wholly good nor wholly evil and, if misguided, at least not beyond the reach of reason.

It follows that a half-truth — that is to say, an abstract description capable of partial acceptance by both parties to a dispute — offers a fifty per cent chance of an agreed solution. And, in the third quarter of the twentieth century, a fifty per cent chance is a sound commercial risk.

There is, however, one possible objection to the theory of terminal situations which may hitherto have been given insufficient weight. Its essence is the supposed need to accord priority to long-term rather than short-term interests. It can often be argued that a particular solution to a given dispute, though attainable and immediately advantageous, would not merely expose the government concerned to the risk of subsequent and more serious disputes, but that the very nature of this first solution would increase the difficulty of finding any satisfactory issue to the later disputes. This was, for instance, the core of the controversy that raged and, among historians, still rages, over British policy towards

Germany during the thirties. The point that concerns us here is not a straightforward weighing of immediate advantage against its ultimate cost. This entails no more than extending our choice of terminal situations a little further into the future. When Germany occupied the Rhineland, for instance, Baldwin concentrated his attention on the solution of the particular dispute thus initiated; Churchill looked further ahead, regarding this incident as only the opening move in a larger and more protracted quarrel. Each based his judgement on a comparison of terminal situations, but the time-scale was different because they judged German intentions differently. Baldwin thought his preferred solution would end the dispute, whereas Churchill correctly predicted that this would only extend it.

This problem of the time-scale is one on which the theory of terminal situations offers no guidance of general application. When the decision is taken to work for a particular terminal situation, certainty is seldom possible that even the achievement of that situation will actually constitute the end of the dispute. Seven years after the Cuban crisis it looks as if the withdrawal of Russian missiles and the lifting of the American naval blockade did, indeed, end that particular dispute. Nor does it appear, whether one tries to regard the subsequent course of events with the eyes of Moscow or those of Washington, that the conclusion of this dispute sowed the seeds of fresh quarrels or aggravated the tension existing between the Soviet Union and the United States. On the contrary, in so far as the later repercussions of this event can be traced or distinguished from those of other developments, these seem to have been of benefit to both governments, whose relationship has perceptibly increased in stability as a result of the new awareness of one another's intentions so painfully acquired in that dramatic confrontation.

These, however, are results which it would have been hard to predict with confidence even in December 1962. Many observers feared at the time – and similar apprehensions must surely have been felt in Moscow – that Mr. Rusk's conclusion – 'the Russians flinched' – would be widely shared in the United States and lead American policy-makers into hazardous and over-confident courses. Others – unable to credit Mr. Khruschev's rationalization of the outcome as the triumph of Soviet policy – foresaw a growing Russian resolve to avenge their humiliation. There were even Americans, hard though this seems to believe today, to whom the outcome represented an American defeat as certain to incur disastrous consequences as Chamberlain's appeasement of Nazi Germany.

At the time it was naturally easier for Khruschev and Kennedy to dismiss such gloomy predictions as deserving less attention than the stark alternatives that emerged from a comparison of more immediate terminal situations. In 1936 a decision to risk war might have been disadvantageous, but scarcely disastrous. In 1962 the extreme, immediate and mutually exclusive options were war and survival. In acute crises between Super-Powers the advent of thermo-nuclear weapons has drastically simplified the problem of the time-scale: the choice of immediate terminal situations necessarily receives priority, because a mistake here could eliminate the possibility of a second choice.

Such acute crises, however, are mercifully rare and, in the majority of disputes, it is still possible for governments to be confronted by two sets of choices which compel them to weigh short-term gains against long-term losses and vice versa. In such cases the trend of previous arguments would be towards basing the decision on a balance of advantage weighted by a balance of probabilities. As long-term developments are inherently less predictable, the result would be a perceptible bias in favour of short-term gains. But each dispute would demand separate consideration in the light of the purposes, resources and intentions of the contestants. If the intentions — and the capacities — of one government suggested that the dispute would be prolonged beyond any immediate terminal situation, the other government would have to raise their sights and adjust their time-scale accordingly.

This is the approach recommended in the present work, because it is directed to the Reality of problems as expressed in their terminal situations. It is, however, heavily dependent on the difficult and uncertain processes of prediction, both primary and secondary, so that there will always be strong inducements to seek some formula that might enable statesmen to escape, or at least to simplify, this exacting and dangerous task. Hence the continuing attraction, even to reasonable men, of the Apparent aspects of disputes, where the simpler slogans of Justice, Honour, Good Faith, Resistance to Aggression and the like seem to offer convenient short-cuts to decision. There is no need to recapitulate earlier arguments against these one-sided formulations, but there may still be a case for considering other, and more neutral, abstractions. Although Russia's 'standing' was too subjective a concept to provide a useful basis for secondary prediction, it did prove practicable to forecast the indirect and remoter repercussions of Russian action in terms of the arousal of hope or fear. These were concepts that could be employed by governments of different preconceptions to reach a broadly similar assessment. But they were also pointers to a terminal situation: a state of affairs in which, for certain governments, the Soviet Union would be a source of increased hope or fear. The intensity of these emotions and their practical expression were expected to vary considerably from one government to another, but questions concerning hope and fear were at least aids to prediction, though not substitutes for the individual assessment of terminal situations.

Is there no abstraction of less limited and particular application, a touchstone, however rough and ready, that would indicate the general balance of advantage to be expected from making one choice rather than another? Businessmen are fond of preaching — perhaps less fond of practising — that 'honesty is the best policy': is there no similar and more objective precept for Foreign Secretaries?

One concept often discussed is that of reliability: the idea that the actions of a particular government produce indirect advantage to the extent that they encourage others to believe that promises will be kept and threats implemented. The initial cost of acquiring such a reputation may be considerable, but thereafter great economies may be achieved through the ability to substitute words for deeds. This is a concept with obvious affinities to predictability, earlier noted as an important factor in the maintenance of international stability.

It has, however, one obvious disadvantage: it is peculiarly susceptible of subjective interpretation. At any given moment the reliability of the British Government will be very differently estimated in London and in other capitals. When the British Government consider they have done all that could reasonably be expected of them, there is always some foreigner to cry, sometimes not without a degree of plausibility, 'perfide Albion'.

Nevertheless this is a concept that occupies so prominent a position in the works of the classical writers upon international affairs as to deserve further examination here. It may conveniently be considered under two aspects: prestige and influence. Prestige may be termed the negative aspect, in that it is a concept which, whatever its potential value, presents itself primarily as an asset requiring constant effort for its maintenance. Influence, on the other hand, is the intangible factor expected to tip the balance in situations where an assessment confined to more concrete elements might not indicate a favourable terminal situation. Both, in the eyes of their proponents, possess a significance not confined to any particular dispute or even to any given phase of international relations. Theoretical concepts, however, always benefit from the application of practical tests. In the two following chapters, therefore, an attempt will be made to test and examine each of these abstractions in the light of particular instances of their application.

5

APPLICATIONS AND ILLUSIONS
OF PRESTIGE IN ASIA

'The festal blazes, the triumphal show
The ravish'd standard and the captive foe,
The Senate's thanks, the Gazette's pompous tale
With force resistless o'er the brave prevail.
Such bribes the rapid Greek o'er Asia whirled,
For such the steady Roman shook the world;
For such in distant lands the Britons shine'

Johnson[1]

THERE are two reasons for concentrating on Asia
in any attempt to explore the practical implications
of prestige: that was the theatre of its most conspicuous
historical exercise and that is also the continent in which
prestige is still a topical issue. The word is less often
employed today, but in 1969 the concept was still one
of those underlying the protracted negotiations for an
end of the war in Vietnam. Certain solutions, it could
be argued, would either augment or diminish the prestige
enjoyed by the United States in the eyes of client nations,
of more independent allies, of hostile powers or of uncommitted countries. The damage to American prestige,
for instance, might outweigh the advantages of an
otherwise attractive terminal situation.

[1] Samuel Johnson, 'The Vanity of Human Wishes'.

139

This is an aspect worth emphasizing at the outset of a chapter which, because of its concentration on a period of history and a pattern of international relationships somewhat remote from the contemporary scene, might otherwise seem lacking in the immediate relevance of the more recent instances selected in earlier passages. Analysts of the pressing problems of the moment are often tempted to assume that the pages of the past have been irrevocably turned and no longer offer any useful lesson in the utterly altered circumstances of today. They are right to be suspicious of the facile use of historical analogy — the moral of Munich, for instance, has been lamentably and dangerously overworked. But relevance depends on similarity of situation and, if this exists, is not necessarily diminished by the mere passage of time.

If American prestige in Asia is, as has often been suggested, now at stake, it may thus be no less useful to examine this concept at its zenith in the same region than to consider more recent, but otherwise less similar applications. Nevertheless, although the discussion that follows may be relevant to the issues arising over Vietnam, this remains an essentially general and theoretical analysis. It is not the purpose of this chapter to consider the merits, in relation to Vietnam, of any particular arguments or to speculate on the circumstances in which they might be invoked, but to attempt a brief analysis of the concept of prestige and, by examining certain aspects of its earlier application in Asia, to see whether any theoretical principles emerge which might be relevant to the choices likely to confront American negotiators.

Prestige is among the most potent, and the least precise, of the many abstractions which, to the dismay of the scientist and the bewilderment of the businessman, continue to dominate the deplorably unquantified discussion of international disputes. The very word is often enough to inspire a warm glow of approval or an instinctive retch of aversion. These are irrelevant reactions. If the concept is useful, it is as a shorthand symbol, a significant contraction of a valid chain of reasoning. To understand it, to use it, to control it, the word must be stripped of its emotional overtones and the concept must be dispassionately examined, neither as a virtue nor as a vice, but as a tool, an instrument to the hand of potentially rational governments.

The first step is to define the context. Prestige will be considered here as one of the expedients which are employed by nation-states to maintain an authority or influence extending beyond their own borders. The desirability of this objective, which has dominated the policies of many nations at different times, is not in question here: we are concerned with means not ends. The history of Asia in the century before 1941 is particularly rich in examples of the extended employment of this technique, but their relevance to contemporary American preoccupations in Vietnam does not depend on a continental coincidence. Any principles which can be derived from past events in Asia should be capable of wider application. It is not only in that continent that the United States Government seek to exercise authority or influence, nor are the Americans the only people now nourishing such ambitions. Egypt is as concerned to maintain and extend her predominance in the Arab world as the Soviet Union in Eastern Europe or France in Western. If the concept of prestige was useful in the past, its contemporary applications deserve study; if it was formerly an illusion, it could become one again.

But emotion must be resisted: it is the dictionary that must guide us. Prestige is the influence acquired by past achievement or, more precisely in this particular context, by a reputation for successful persistence in the enforcement of demands, in the implementation of threats and in the fulfilment of undertakings. Ideally the words of a government with such a reputation are regarded as a reliable prelude to deeds and come to be accepted as their equivalent, just as paper money can seem worth the gold it promises. The more prestige a government enjoys the greater its ability to influence the actions of others without resort to either coercion or material reward. Internally, of course, this is an elementary proposition. Civilization depends on the readiness of most citizens to obey laws without bribes or a gun at their heads. It is in the exertion of authority over foreigners, over people with no inherent incentive for compliance, that the value of prestige, of a reputation for getting one's own way in the end, deserves the attention alike of the political scientist and of the practical man of affairs.

This was a concept which preoccupied the makers of British policy in Asia for much of the nineteenth and early twentieth centuries, but there was one country and one period in which the actual results of prestige were so demonstrable as to be almost quantifiable. From 1858 to 1939 the British ruled India with resources that most governments would have considered grossly inadequate for the maintenance of public order within their own boundaries:

> 'There was about one British soldier and four Indian soldiers in India to every six thousand of the population. In most districts there were no British soldiers; in very many there were no soldiers at all, British or Indian. There might be none within a hundred, two hundred or three hundred miles. There might be seven or eight hundred police in a district to a million or so inhabitants; they would all be Indian . . .'
>
> 'In 1909 the provincial government consisted of a Governor, three secretaries and three under-secretaries – seven men . . . population was then roughly that of Great Britain.'
>
> 'It was felt safe to reduce the number of British troops throughout India to fifteen thousand . . . among three hundred million . . .'
>
> 'Since 1919 there had been an increase of 44 officers in the Indian Civil Service, the total rising from 1255 to 1299 (in 1939). This was for the three and a half hundred million of India.'[1]

These figures are sufficiently startling when viewed in isolation. But if they are compared with the 250,000 soldiers employed in 1968 to reassert Russian influence over the Czechoslovak Communist Party or with the 437,000 American soldiers, the countless auxiliaries and the huge air and naval forces which failed to restore the authority of the Government of South Vietnam or, lest British complacency be unduly fostered, with the 84,000 British soldiers who could not keep order among less than two million inhabitants of Palestine during the last years of the British Mandate, the discrepancy becomes overwhelming. How did such minute forces,

[1] Philip Woodruff, *The Men Who Ruled India* (Jonathan Cape 1954).

such a handful of administrators, assert a dominance seldom questioned by hundreds of millions of Indians? Why, to employ Lord Curzon's words, did this 'little foam on an unfathomable and dark ocean' not merely subdue India with greater economy and efficacity than her own rulers have subsequently achieved, but also serve as one of the twin pillars – the other was the Royal Navy – of a system of imperialism that stretched from the Persian Gulf to the navigable limits of the great rivers of China? Why has no other government – not even those of the dauntingly equipped and rightly named Super-Powers – since imitated this effortless assertion of external authority?

There are more answers to this question than can be considered here and it would be misleading to suggest prestige or other political factors as the sole explanation. But governments exist to exercise authority and an abstraction which even assists an alien government to rule three hundred and fifty million Indians with an establishment of British man-power little greater than that deployed on 27 October 1968 to control a single Vietnam demonstration in London is surely deserving of dispassionate examination.

One misconception must be disposed of at the outset. It is often argued that European ascendancy in Asia was based on the insuperable military advantages conferred by a more advanced technology and that such political factors as existed were then secondary and, in a different technological era, are now irrelevant. This is a proposition most easily argued in relation to the incursions of the sixteenth century, when European vessels arriving in Asian waters could not be matched for the power and the number of the cannon they carried.[1] Although gunpowder had been known in Asia since the tenth century and cannon since at least the fourteenth, their employment in war and their manufacture had never been practised on the same scale as in Europe and only the Japanese and Koreans had hitherto had much experience of their use in naval battles. In the China Sea and the Indian Ocean sea-borne artillery on the European scale was a military innovation of the first importance and one which could scarcely be countered except by a prolonged and laborious process of acquiring the new skills needed to construct and employ this relatively advanced type of ordnance. Time and the absence of external interference were obviously indispensable conditions and could easily have been denied by a rapid extension of European power in Asia, in which case the subsequent course of history might reasonably have been described as the result of the overwhelming advantages conferred by superior technology.

This was not, however, what actually happened. Two and a half centuries after the Portuguese had first demonstrated the significance of naval gunnery in Asian waters — a demonstration that was constantly repeated — the European intruders were still clinging precariously to a handful of forts and trading posts scattered along the shores of the Asian mainland. Only in parts of the Malay archipelago was their survival at all independent of the continued favour of local rulers and nowhere in continental Asia had they posed a serious challenge to existing territorial authority. The potentates of China

[1] See Carlo M. Cipolla, *Guns, Sails and Empires* (Pantheon 1965) for a scholarly exposition and a lavish bibliography.

and India had been afforded ample time to reorganize their defences and many of them are known to have recognized the need and the means. If the numerous efforts actually made during this period to procure cannon and artificers, to establish ordnance foundries and to train artillerymen were never pursued with sufficient vigour or consistency to achieve the results intended, complacency and conservatism were more potent causes than ignorance or technical incapacity.

Nor can the subsequent extension of European power from the high seas to the mainland of Asia be ascribed to a sudden advance in European technology or a further transformation of the established techniques of war. These underwent no fundamental change in the century of conquest after 1750 and the armament employed by the British was still the familiar répertoire of wooden sailing-ships, muzzle-loading cannon and smooth-bore muskets, weapons that could have been – and often were – equally available to both sides. Real technical innovation came later and was not always advantageous to the British: the greased cartridges of the Lee-Enfield rifle precipitated the Indian Mutiny and the only serious challenge to British supremacy during the nineteenth century, while the deficiencies of the Armstrong breech-loading gun were largely responsible for Admiral Kuper's partial repulse at Kagoshima in 1863. Indeed, it is one of the ironies of history that the mid-Victorian era of almost effortless British supremacy in Asia was sustained by an army and a navy at one of their lowest ebbs in modernity of equipment or technical proficiency and that the subsequent surge of military innovation was to coincide with the beginning of the end for an Empire that had owed much to the British armed forces, but little to their possession of weapons not available to their enemies.

A second error should not, but does, deserve an equal refutation. Even in past centuries the British people had no inherent advantage in courage or the other martial virtues. Half a dozen years before Clive's first victory over superior forces at Arcot, regular English regiments had, in two successive battles, run in broken panic before the charge of the Highland clans. Only in the third, on Drummossie Muir, had organization, discipline and a cohesive nationalism defeated the primitive levies of a small fraction of a deeply divided Scotland. It was these essentially political forces, the characteristics of a fully developed nation-state, that prevailed over the anarchy and factionalism of Asia's inchoate social structures. Few peoples can even be compared with the Japanese for disciplined bravery, but their forts fell to British sailors because the Japan of the eighteen sixties was politically neither united nor organized. Admittedly the British – and the other European conquerors of Asia during the eighteenth and nineteenth centuries – were possessed by an amazing *Wille zur Macht*, but they succeeded because they were united by a common determination, whereas their more numerous opponents were divided, unorganized, indecisive, often indifferent and sometimes collaborators. In Vietnam some may consider that this balance of political advantage has been reversed since 1945.

Prestige, however, belongs to the latter half of the nineteenth century. It did not, could not, exist in the era of conquest, when even an educated Indian ruler in alliance with the French (Suraj-ud-Daula) could believe that Europe had no more than ten thousand inhabitants.[1] It was the long succession of British victories, the stubborn perseverance with which they returned after every setback, the continuity and persistence of their rule, which finally established in Asian minds that sense of inevitability which is the essence of prestige.[2] Citizens do not pay income-tax because they like it or, in most cases, because they think it right and just: they pay it because they are convinced there is no escape from this vexatious obligation. In the end they will be made to pay, so the majority prefer, with whatever reluctance and disgust, to do so at the beginning.

This is a point often missed by critics of the concept of prestige. Panikkar, for instance, sometimes treats prestige as if it meant only the pomp and circumstance and outward show of authority. He argues that the British made themselves ludicrous and unpopular in India by their insistence on a superior social status expressed in their style of living, the number of their servants and the elaborate etiquette governing their relations with Indians. He may be right.[3] But, when he

[1] This was 200 years ago, but, even in 1842, the Chinese addressed Queen Victoria as 'chieftainess of the tribe' – Panikkar, *Asia and Western Dominance* (Allen & Unwin 1953).

[2] Not long after the bombardment of Shimonoseki Japanese officials urged the Court: 'let the foolish argument which has hitherto styled foreigners dogs and goats and barbarians be abandoned.' Morse & MacNair, *Far Eastern International Relations* (Boston, Houghton Mifflin 1931).

[3] Nevertheless distinctive privileges have always attracted governments as an economical form of reward. This is often resented. One result of the 1956 revolution in Hungary, for instance, was the withdrawal from senior Communist officials of the privilege of having their car windows curtained against the gaze of the vulgar, a distinction perhaps as curious in itself as in the indignation it aroused.

goes on to suggest that 'a reputation for goodness and holiness' would have conferred greater prestige, he mistakes the meaning of the word. Prestige is a concept that inspires awe rather than affection or reverence. The social pretensions of British officials – and still more those of their wives and of the British commercial community – may well have been as exaggerated and unnecessary as Chinese insistence on humiliating Ambassadors or denying foreign residents the right to use a sedan chair. But, as long as these were effectively enforced, they were capable, to however trivially an auxiliary extent, of contributing to prestige and thus to the acceptance of authority. Most of the demands by which the British acquired, extended and maintained their influence in Asia can be attacked as absurd or immoral: what matters was whether or not they were enforced. If they were, prestige was increased by the evidence of success; if not, it was diminished. Indeed, this is implicitly recognized by Panikkar himself. Having surveyed, with invariable moral reprobation, the history of European intervention in China during the latter half of the nineteenth century, he concludes that these disreputable acts had created 'the heyday of Western authority in China'. But, when he comes to the period following the First World War, he notes that the substitution of mild protests and patient negotiation for the earlier 'display of overwhelming naval strength' had resulted in a sudden eclipse of European prestige.[1]

In their political relationships human beings are primarily actuated by hope and fear: prestige is a device for the economical maintenance of these sentiments. Its

[1] Panikkar, op. cit.

foundation is reliability. Allies, ambassadors, district officers and policemen must be able to hope with confidence that their loyalty will be rewarded and supported. Enemies, foreign governments, the disaffected and seditious must have good reason to fear that their defiance will bring retribution. In the long run the operation of such a system offers great economies, because the government enjoying prestige can often employ words to obtain advantages for which less fortunate governments would have to pay in hard cash or the blood of their soldiers.

Once the ascendancy of the British had been established and, by a century of repeated victories, confirmed, peace, efficient and uncorrupt administration, a uniform system of law and political stability prevailed throughout the British Empire in Asia and encouraged the prosperity of British commerce at the minimum cost to the British taxpayer. Never before or since have the inhabitants of this area enjoyed so much security for their lives and property at so little expense in the maintenance of armed forces, police and administrative services. Nor were these benefits accompanied by a degree of political repression at all comparable with that since instituted by many independent Asian governments. As long as the British people wanted an Empire in Asia, the careful cultivation of British prestige, even when this involved actions that might in themselves be regarded as discreditable, disadvantageous or irrational, constituted a policy as effective as it was economical.

But prestige has its price. The reliability of the authority mirrored by prestige must be unremitting. Allies must be supported even if their cause is bad;

unreasonable demands, once made, must be enforced; officials must be upheld even in their errors of judgement. Such decisions are liable to attract criticism and the natural sensitivity of democratic governments to their own public opinion is often reinforced because the economies of prestige are only apparent over a period: at the moment when action is taken to uphold it, only the expense is obvious. It may be true that the early use of force often saves more lives than it costs; that naval superiority is cheaper than a war; that the greatest sufferings of humanity have never resulted from the regular assertion of authority, but from the explosions of violence that follow its neglect or decay. But all these propositions require governments to embrace immediate evil, however limited, in order to secure ultimate good. This is often a difficult course to defend in public debate and, given the inevitable fallibility of human prediction, it is also an argument which has often been wrongly applied. The ultimate results of using force did not always outweigh their immediate disadvantages even in nineteenth-century Asia.

This is perhaps a weakness inseparable from any consistent policy directed towards long-term objectives. Errors will occur, but, if the general trend of decisions and their results is as favourable as was the case with British imperial rule in Asia, may be accepted. A more serious flaw in the concept of prestige is its tendency to assume intrinsic rather than auxiliary importance in the minds of those who apply it. In this it resembles credit: an admirable substitute for barter or the transfer of precious metals, but one which can not, without disastrous results, be inflated or prolonged regardless of the limits set by the concrete transactions of which it is only the abstract symbol. Prestige can augment the advantages to be derived from power and temporarily conceal its deficiencies, but prestige can neither precede power nor long survive its cessation.

This is a weakness doubly illustrated by British relations with China. To begin with, it was the Chinese who mistakenly relied on prestige as a substitute for a power they did not possess. Accustomed as they were – until nearly the end of the nineteenth century – to receive tokens of tribute and submission from neighbouring states over which they had long ceased to exercise effective control, they were obsessed by the notion that the mere maintenance of Chinese prestige would enable them to assert their authority over foreign barbarians of every description. When Lord Macartney brought the greetings of King George III to the Emperor of China, the Chinese escort who accompanied him to Peking took care to display a banner reading 'Ambassador bearing tribute from the country of England' and a later Ambassador had to withdraw without presenting his credentials because the Chinese insisted on his performing the kowtow appropriate to a vassal. The first century of European relations with China was characterized – and many of its conflicts provoked – by Chinese pursuit of a policy of prestige which demanded that foreigners should recognize their inferior status by prostrating themselves, by presenting 'petitions' rather than letters and by not walking on the streets.

This policy failed because it could not be enforced. The Chinese lacked the organization and the unity to exclude from their country the foreigners who sought intercourse on terms of equality. But, although the British – and other nations – succeeded in forcing themselves into China, their efforts to establish their position in the country on a basis of prestige alone were equally unsuccessful. In 1847 Lord Palmerston's principles were unexceptionable:

> 'We shall lose all the vantage ground we have gained by our victories in China, if we take a low tone. We must take especial care not to descend from the relative position we have acquired. If we maintain that position morally, by the tone of our intercourse, we shall not be obliged to recover it by forcible acts; but if we permit the Chinese, either at Canton or elsewhere, to resume, as they will no doubt always be endeavouring to do so, their former tone of affected superiority, we shall very soon be compelled to come to blows with them again . . . the Chinese must learn and be convinced, that if they attack our people and our factories, they will be shot.'[1]

These precepts were applied, with commendable consistency, during the following century, but successive British governments were constantly 'compelled to come to blows with them again': British influence in China could only be maintained by the repeated use of force, was given its death-blow by the Japanese victories and finally expired as soon as force was conclusively shown – by the *Amethyst* incident of 1949 – to be no longer feasible. It is true that remarkable victories were repeatedly won by inferior forces and that the Chinese often made concessions disproportionate to the military pressures exerted upon them. It may well be argued that the reputation derived from each victory made the next easier and that, but for a consistent policy of building

[1] Quoted in Morse & MacNair, op. cit.

prestige, the slender forces employed would never have been able repeatedly to impose alien demands on so vast and hostile, if disorganized, a people. It is also true that, for most of this period, small communities and even isolated British subjects were scattered throughout the length and breadth of China and maintained, however precariously, their independent and even privileged existence in a manner now inconceivable. Again and again, however, British warships had to be summoned or British expeditionary forces landed to rescue the bare lives of British subjects from the xenophobic fury of the Chinese among whom they lived. And, all too often, these rescuers arrived too late to do more than enforce retribution on the assailants.

In so brief a reference to so long, so complex and so controversial a chapter of British imperialism, it is difficult to strike a balance or to hazard an opinion on the genuine contribution of prestige over and above the repeated intervention of small and disciplined forces in a country perpetually distracted by civil war. But it is worth remembering that, even if the Royal Navy had to appoint an officer with the remarkable title of Rear-Admiral YANGTSE to control the operations of British warships protecting British subjects a thousand miles inside China, the Navy also indicated their notion of what might be expected of the mere influence and prestige of British Consuls by requesting them not to interfere with manœuvres by calling for gun-boats between March and October.[1] Lord Palmerston's expectations were not fulfilled; the Chinese never accepted the inevitability of the presence in their midst of the

[1] Hewlett, *Forty Years in China* (Macmillan 1943).

British barbarians; there was never a time when British diplomatic and consular representatives did not need to be familiar with the whereabouts and availability of the nearest British armed forces. Nevertheless, if one examines the history of the penultimate period – the twenties – it is arguable that British influence in China was more effective than that of Japan or the United States and that, as both these countries then enjoyed greater power in Asia, this discrepancy was only attributable to the legacy of British prestige.

China, however, is at best a doubtful case. Prestige could never be fully effective there, because prestige is no more than the reflection, albeit enhanced, of power. And power is itself another abstraction: the ability to apply definitive, or at least purposeful, force at the decisive point and the critical moment.[1] The value of latent power depends on its acceptance. Unless the capacity to compel obedience is recognized, it can offer no alternative to the constant use or threat of actual force. This recognition was extended by the Government of Japan, who proceeded first to secure their own internal authority and then to establish with the British – and other foreigners – a relationship on the basis of that equality they had themselves initially denied. Similar recognition was forthcoming from the Government of Thailand, from whom the British obtained substantial concessions without the use of force, and from the directly ruled peoples of the British Empire in Asia. But Chinese recognition of British ability to enforce initially modest claims was never lastingly conceded and, as the British tended to make new claims after each armed intervention

---

[1] For further discussion of these ideas, see Grant Hugo, op. cit.

to enforce those earlier denied, there was never a period of acquiescent stability long enough to demonstrate the full operation of prestige as a substitute for actual force.

There did develop, however, an illusion of prestige and a fundamental misconception of its relation to power. Because British armed intervention in China had so long achieved a success out of all proportion to the forces available to the contestants, the British had come to take it for granted that they could and should do whatever they pleased in China. They forgot the extent to which their dominance depended on essentially political factors: superior national unity, organization and discipline. They forgot, above all, that these political advantages were not immutable. They accordingly involved themselves in one of the oddest and most revealing of mid-twentieth century misadventures: the affair of H.M.S. *Amethyst*, the frigate which failed to reach Nanking in 1949 after being attacked, while on passage up the Yangtse, by field-guns of the Chinese Communist Army, but which subsequently escaped and rejoined the fleet. This incident has often been criticized on purely military grounds by people who forget that four British gun-boats were sunk in an unsuccessful attack on the Taku forts in 1860. It was nothing new for British warships to expose themselves to artillery in the confined space of Chinese rivers and the purely military risks run by H.M.S. *Amethyst* were no greater than those often surmounted by her predecessors. What was different was a degree of Chinese organization capable of concentrating the rudimentary forces needed to make an opposed ascent of Chinese rivers impossible. What was odd was the British assumption that their residual prestige would induce the Communists to refrain from exploiting their obvious military advantage; what was odder still was that the Communists did, from whatever motive, reveal themselves as willing to wound, but reluctant to strike home. On 21 April 1949 naval reinforcements had failed to rescue a ship which was partially crippled and had lost half her crew. Further shelling would have quickly sunk her; a determined boarding-party might even have captured her in an immediate night attack. Yet H.M.S. *Amethyst* remained unmolested and the subject of negotiation – was even partially revictualled with Communist consent – until 30 July, when she made her famous escape.

Why? Nothing in the prior – or subsequent – conduct of the Chinese Communist leaders suggests that humanity, moderation, anxiety to conciliate world opinion or concern for the conventions of international law are especially prominent among their motives. No rational analysis of the situation in 1949 could have indicated that there was much to be feared from British resentment. What could the British have done if a few hours of steady shelling had destroyed H.M.S. *Amethyst* on 21 April? We may never know the true explanation, but it is at least conceivable that the strange bubble prestige had first led this frigate into a militarily impossible situation[1] and had then enabled her to escape. Perhaps there was a lingering, an unfounded, an irrational conviction

---

[1] This was by no means the first such error. Fifty years earlier the British Prime Minister was complaining of 'that phase of British temper which in the last few months has led detachment after detachment of British troops into the most obvious ambuscades – mere arrogance'. Quoted in Grenville, *Lord Salisbury and Foreign Policy* (Athlone Press 1964).

that if the Chinese 'attack our people – they will be shot'.

What conclusions can be drawn from this hasty and incomplete survey of the applications and illusions of a vanished British prestige in Asia? The first, surely, is that the creation of prestige demands a long period of relatively unbroken success in the exercise of power. It is not to be achieved in a decade and, if Admiral Cunningham exaggerated in his famous dictum that 'it only takes three years to build a ship: it takes three hundred to create a tradition', it was probably, even amid the political acceleration of today, only by a factor of ten. The second is that prestige does not only reflect power, but the acceptance of power, and that this acceptance depends as much on the political as on the military balance of advantage. These two conclusions lead to a third: that prestige is most important in those international relationships of which both sides recognize the inequality. Prestige seems to have exercised little influence on British relations with countries, whether in Asia or outside it, that were at all comparable in power and political development. As early as 1901, for instance, even those Japanese then advocating alliance with Britain had to admit that the 'national influence of Great Britain has already passed its peak and is slightly on the decline'.[1] This was the cool comment of an equal and the next few decades made it brutally clear that, wherever else British prestige might still inspire a lingering awe, the Japanese based their assessments solely on the disposable resources and apparent resolve of successive British governments.

[1] Quoted in Grenville, op. cit.

If these conclusions are correct, then the second half of the twentieth century is singularly ill suited to the cultivation of prestige and, even if this effort had been attempted by the United States, might have proved beyond even their great resources. In fact the United States have never pursued – at any rate for long enough to be effective – a policy of prestige. Their attitudes in Asia were decided *ad hoc* and on other principles: there was no consistent policy or pattern of behaviour. Whether the United States abstained, as over Manchuria in 1931, or intervened, as over Korea in 1950, American decisions were apt to come as a genuine surprise to foreigners. Before and after the Second World War American influence in Asia has required an individual effort at coercion or inducement on each separate occasion of its assertion. There has been no tradition of consistent American determination to enforce their authority which might have obviated the exercise of power or supplied its occasional deficiencies. Compare, for instance, the *Amethyst* incident of 1949 – that last flicker of an already extinguished British prestige – with the *Pueblo* incident of 1968.

It follows that American prestige is not an issue in Vietnam, because that prestige, in the sense here considered, does not now exist. There is no additional element of American authority, over and above the concrete foundations of power and wealth, to be impaired by concessions; no long-nurtured tradition of inevitable success to be destroyed by failure. American policy does not enjoy the extra advantages derived from the maintenance of a prestige system, but nor is it vulnerable to the penalties of that system: there is no artificial and precarious bubble to be burst by a single setback.

When people talk,[1] as they do, of the risks to American prestige in Vietnam, they are thinking of something else: that American concessions there might be regarded by other governments as creating a precedent and might thus, on some different and future occasion, cause foreigners to under-estimate the power of the United States and their readiness to stand by their allies and clients. This is a distinction with a difference. One of the reasons why unredeemed failure is automatically fatal to prestige is that foreigners regard the maintenance of prestige as the primary objective of the government enjoying it: failure can accordingly only be ascribed to a deficiency either of power or else of resolve. The motives of the United States Government, however, are known to be more complex; they are constantly ventilated in public debate; they are as assiduously analysed in Hanoi and Moscow and Peking as in London or Paris. Indeed this very openness of American policy, its democratic malleability, has perhaps been the major obstacle to the creation of American prestige, which would have demanded a degree of reliability and consistency scarcely to be achieved by a government compelled to be constantly responsive to the vagaries of public opinion. As a result foreigners are accustomed to the need for a fresh appraisal of American power and resolve on the occasion of every new crisis. American staunchness over Berlin in 1958 came as no surprise to those who had witnessed,

[1] '..."prestige" is not an empty word.... If we simply abandoned our effort in Vietnam, the cause of peace might not survive the damage that would be done to other nations' confidence in our reliability.' — President Nixon, broadcast address, 15 May 1969.

whether with delight or dismay, her different conduct over Suez in 1956. Experienced observers realize that for the United States, as for other countries, circumstances alter cases. There is no reason why American concessions in Vietnam, if circumstances were to make these intrinsically desirable, should have any more effect on the respect inspired by American attitudes in some future crisis than did Soviet concessions over Cuba in 1962.

Indeed, if anyone's prestige is at stake in Vietnam, it is Ho Chi Minh's. Thirty years of utter consistency have brought him success and influence out of all proportion either to his relative power or to the extent of his actual military victories. But that, as Kipling used to say, is another story. The hands of the American negotiators will be neither strengthened nor fettered by prestige. For them it will have no application: may they also be free of its illusions.

6

INFLUENCE WITHOUT POWER

'What is more, and, as I believe, much more, there is a sense
in which the very difficulties and dangers that we face en-
hance our inherent spiritual strength. We speak in the modern
world with nothing less than commanding moral authority.'

Hailsham[1]

IF, in the modern world, prestige must be reluctantly
abandoned as a paper currency discredited by the
disappearance of any automatic acceptance of latent
power as the standard of international relationships,
there is the more need to scrutinize the possibility of its
replacement by influence.

The influence enjoyed by a nation-state beyond its
borders has, admittedly, been traditionally regarded as a
function of its power. Such power is not necessarily
military. Wealth and financial acumen have earned for
the Swiss a degree of influence on the world's economy
envied by many nations with no cause to consider the
armed forces of Switzerland. It is in the money markets
of the world that Swiss ability to reward or punish is
recognized and it is this recognition, by its maintenance
in others of those sentiments of hope and fear which
most frequently and reliably determine the actions of
governments, that constitutes the basis of influence
derived from power.

[1] Viscount Hailsham, *The Conservative Case*, Penguin 1959.

This kind of influence is naturally not the result of resources alone, but also of the way in which these resources are exploited. The intelligent and consistent use of power can augment, as its neglect or erratic application can diminish, the extent of an influence which does not depend only on the recognition that power exists, but also on the expectation that it will actually be employed. Ten times as much money would not give the Swiss their present influence if these funds remained inert rather than in perpetually restless search of greater profit and security.

Nevertheless the traditional theory maintains that policy determines only the ratio between basic power and resultant influence. The best of policies can not create influence without any foundation of power, nor inflate it beyond all proportion, nor long preserve it once the originating power has dwindled.

This is a contention often challenged by those who prefer to seek the sources of influence in the ability to inspire affection, esteem or loyalty. They argue that a government professing ideas or principles attractive to other people will acquire a corresponding influence over their actions; or that a government with a reputation for benevolence and efficiency at home will be respected and followed abroad; or that similarities in customs, institutions, language or religion will be reflected in policies; that influence is the reward of merit or the natural result of coincident opinions. Influence, in this view, can exist independently of power and can provide an alternative means of advancing national objectives.

These arguments have always commanded an audience in Britain, but their attractions have increased with the uneasy consciousness of the last two decades that British influence over the actions of foreign governments has visibly declined. Even those who accept the traditional view and explain this phenomenon as the inevitable result of Britain's reduced capacity to punish or reward are tempted by the idea that other sources of influence could be developed with less difficulty, expense and inconvenience than would necessarily be entailed by the effort to restore Britain's relative power. Before examining any such alternatives, however, it is important to be clear about the true nature and meaning of influence in international affairs: the ability to persuade a foreign government to do something which they would not otherwise have done.

This is a more complex and difficult proposition than may at first be obvious, for it involves more than a comparison between the request made of a foreign government and their response. Refusal may only indicate a conflict of interests too fundamental to be overcome by persuasion from any quarter; compliance may only be due to realization that a common interest exists. In neither case can the result be regarded as a fair test of influence. Moreover, the motives of any particular governmental decision are not always obvious: what appears to spring from the success or failure of influence may actually have quite other causes.

There are, however, certain rough and ready methods of assessing influence. One is to examine the results of a series of representations made to a particular foreign government, about the treatment of British subjects in China, for instance. One, or two, or even several of these requests may have been decided on quite other grounds, but a consistent trend towards either rejection or compliance would be evidence of the extent of British influence. Another test is possible when the British Government address the same request to a number of different governments, when the pattern of their responses may be taken as a measure of British influence because the multiplicity of particular motives involved is likely to be self-cancelling. Perhaps the most conveniently quantifiable and comparable of all tests is to analyse the results of voting in the United Nations, particularly on issues in which few of the member-states have any direct interest. Votes are often less important than other decisions, but the very fact that a government can cast a vote without thereby being committed to any consequential action makes that vote easier for others to influence.

For a number of years, for instance, the future of Gibraltar has been the subject of debates and resolutions in the United Nations. In so far as Gibraltar's future could actually be affected by votes in the General Assembly, the repercussions would be directly sustained by only two of the member-states: Britain and Spain. Other governments have not so far had reasonable cause to suppose that their votes would entail any form of concrete action or to expect material loss or gain from either the continuation or the modification of the present state of affairs in Gibraltar. Indirect interests and associated sentiments naturally existed in abundance, but few of these were so strong or so obviously committed to one side or the other as to leave no scope for the exertion of influence. Both Britain and Spain have thus repeatedly solicited, whether in open debate or through diplomatic representations, the votes of other members in support of their respective arguments. In doing so each could probably count on a hard core of partisans: it is difficult to imagine popular sentiment permitting the government of New Zealand to support Spain or that of Argentina to ignore the analogy between the Spanish claim to Gibraltar and their own to the Falkland Islands.

But, whether one compares British and Spanish arguments or examines the affiliations and previous voting records of the governments taking part, it would be difficult to regard this as an issue in which more than a small minority of the United Nations were from the outset necessarily and irreversibly committed. The majority were open to influence and, if a remarkably heterogeneous majority consistently voted against Britain, this can only signify the failure of British influence. Greece, Iran, Italy, the Philippines, Portugal and Turkey are all allied to Britain, but they voted against her on 19 December 1967. Belgium, France, Iceland, the Netherlands, Thailand and the United States are also allies, but they abstained. This was an occasion on which British influence was given a fair test capable of indicating a precise result: 19 votes out of 119.[1]

Most exertions of influence can not be measured with anything approaching this certainty and precision, but nothing deserves the name of influence unless its practical applicability can somehow be demonstrated in terms of decisions taken by foreign governments. General de Gaulle, for instance, has frequently expressed with felicity, and probably with sincerity, his admiration

[1] The voting was 73 against Britain, 19 in favour and 27 abstentions. A further vote in 1968 produced a broadly similar result.

for British institutions and traditions, but he has seldom allowed these sentiments to sway his dispassionate consideration of British diplomatic representations. Similarly, the mere existence of foreigners who speak English, read Shakespeare, admire the National Health Service, spend their holidays in Britain or give their children an English education does not constitute a source of British influence unless these tastes can be shown to affect the decisions of their governments. Influence is the ability to induce action.

In seeking another source than power for effective influence it is also necessary to be sure that there is no hidden element of power prompting the decision of one government to take action in apparent deference to the mere wish of another. This is a factor often overlooked, because the nature of power is so widely misunderstood. Power is only a capacity to punish or reward. It has no intrinsic or universal value and its relevance to any particular situation depends on the extent to which it can actually be applied. The military and economic resources of the United States are superior to those of any other nation, but sometimes prove inadequate to deter some impoverished, defenceless and friendless little country from confiscating American property or maltreating American citizens. In such cases the balance of power depends on a comparison, not of total resources, but of the ease with which each government can apply force to the factory or the person whose fate is at issue. If one can employ a couple of policemen, whereas the other would have to send an amphibious task force, the immediate advantage in terms of power lies with the former and can only be offset if there exists a real expectation that the United States Government will subsequently prove both able and willing to retaliate effectively. If, in such circumstances, the United States Government make some concession, they are doing so in response to an influence based on power, even though that power is purely local and exists only on the assumption that the United States will not consider the effort of its destruction worth the trouble and expense.

Any claim to the exercise of influence unrelated to power thus requires careful scrutiny. In the case of Gibraltar, for instance, the idea that American abstention was influenced by the power of Spain is superficially absurd. On closer examination, however, it is understandable that the United States Government may have regarded Spain as more likely than Britain to punish an adverse vote by withdrawing her consent to the maintenance of American bases or by discriminating against American commercial interests. In real terms, therefore, the advantage of power, and its consequential influence, lay with Spain.

Most examples of influence will thus prove, on careful analysis, to be rooted in the intelligent application of power, even if this power is local, particular, transitory or specialized in character. There are, however, certain governments which, at one time or another during the last two decades, have acquired a reputation for possessing a degree of international influence unrelated to the ordinary or even to the more sophisticated sources of power. China and the Soviet Union, for instance, have sometimes been able to exert an influence derived from the ideological sympathies of individual foreigners; Israel has been able to appeal to the sentiments of racial and religious kinship felt by many foreign Jews; even Britain has benefited from the traditional loyalties of Australians and New Zealanders. Many other examples could be quoted of this kind of indirect influence, in which one government can rely on a particular group of foreign nationals to assist in determining the decisions of their government in the sense desired. All, however, are to some extent fortuitous, in that they depend on the accidents of past history. The Government of Israel did not create an electorally significant concentration of Jews in New York any more than Mr. Brezhnev or Chairman Mao Tse Tung were personally responsible for the existence of Communist theory and its inherent appeal to the discontented of many nations. These were advantages which already existed and which only needed intelligent exploitation.

This kind of influence, though often important, scarcely lends itself to cultivation by the British Government, who can not be expected to develop a new religion or to organize mass emigration on a scale capable of swaying the decisions of those foreign governments whose nationals do not already include a significant proportion claiming British descent. More might perhaps be done to exploit those advantages that already exist. Why, for instance, does Irish political influence in the United States so often appear disproportionate to the ratio between American citizens of Irish and of British descent? But it would hardly be practical to recommend the creation of new international affinities where these do not already exist.

It may thus be preferable to consider those governments which appear to have created their own influence without the benefit of any special prior advantages. Possible examples are: Cambodia, Egypt, Ghana, India, Indonesia and Yugoslavia. Except for Egypt's influence in the Arab world (which is partly based on the accidents of history) none of these governments ever enjoyed an influence as widespread, as decisive or as lasting as that to be derived from power. Outside the Arab world it would be hard to point to many important actions undertaken by others at the mere request of one of these governments. Yugoslavia, for instance, had relatively little success in eliciting even verbal support for her opposition to Russian invasion of Czechoslovakia from any government not already committed to an anti-Russian view. Nevertheless, at various periods each of these governments seemed to enjoy an unusual degree of influence on the kind of decision that can be taken without much regard for immediate consequences. For instance, if Egypt, India or Yugoslavia had decided to vote for Britain in the General Assembly on 19 December 1967, their adhesion would probably have attracted a number of other votes in favour of maintaining the *status quo* in Gibraltar.

As even so minimal a degree of influence would presumably be welcome at present to the British Government, it is worth enquiring further how these governments won their reputation as moulders of uncommitted international opinion and to what extent their methods are susceptible of imitation. To begin with, all these governments were at one time headed by leaders of outstanding individual capacities. Prince Sihanouk, President Nasser, Mr. Nkrumah, Mr. Nehru, Mr. Sukarno, President Tito: these are or were remarkable

men by any political standard. Each succeeded, at least
for a time, in imposing his authority on a people with
little tradition of unity, conformity or homogeneity;
four of them secured important advantages for their
countries; all of them assiduously maintained a personal
claim to the expression of opinions on questions of
international controversy whether or not these directly
involved their respective countries. Indeed, in their
heyday, such utterances were seldom reported as the
views of their governments: it was 'Nasser says . . .' or
'in the words of Nkrumah'. The extent of this purely
personal, this charismatic appeal may be measured by
the diminished influence of Ghana and Indonesia
following the disappearance of Nkrumah and Sukarno
and, to a lesser extent, by the inability of subsequent
Indian leaders to assume the prophetic mantle of
Nehru.

Before concluding from these examples that the
personality of a leader can constitute a source of influence
we need to examine rather more closely the ratio between the ability of these men, at the height of their
ascendancy, to induce action and the resources at their
disposal. The most remarkable case is perhaps that of
Prince Sihanouk. Nehru, after all, was the ruler of one
of the largest countries in the world; President Tito of a
people who had proved themselves in war against a
stronger Power; President Nasser of a nation with the
historical advantage of religious, racial and linguistic
affinities throughout the corners of two continents. Even
the two who ultimately failed had started with great
advantages: Sukarno as the leader of one of the most
populous, vigorous and richly endowed countries in

Asia; Nkrumah with two hundred million pounds in the bank.

But Prince Sihanouk established himself as the leader of a people who, in spite of their ancient traditions, enjoyed none of these assets. They were not rich, numerous, united or renowned for any recent display of martial valour. They were at odds with all their neighbours and, at least for the last two decades, have always included a minority in the more or less active service of foreign governments. In 1954, at the time of the Geneva agreements on the cessation of hostilities in Indo-China, few experts on international affairs would have predicted for Cambodia a fate significantly different from that of Laos or Vietnam. Yet, fourteen years later, Cambodia can boast of a continued peace and prosperity undreamt of by her two neighbours. Nor has this been achieved by constant acquiescence in the demands of the stronger. Prince Sihanouk has successively defied — and sometimes enraged — the governments of China, Great Britain, the Soviet Union, Thailand, the United States and South Vietnam. He has nevertheless succeeded in attracting deference, material assistance or, at the very least, toleration from all of them, to say nothing of a degree of French support never accorded to Laos or Vietnam. Even on the most sophisticated analysis it is difficult to discern any basis of power that could be said to have supported the dexterity of Cambodian manœuvring amid the animosities and conflicting interests of so many governments that were not only potentially stronger, but, in most cases, better able immediately to punish or reward.

The triumph of Prince Sihanouk has not, however,

been limited to the achievement, remarkable though this is, of preserving for fourteen years a peaceful existence for his people. He has also exerted a lesser, but by no means insignificant influence beyond his own borders. Between 1959 and 1961, for instance, the governments of China, Great Britain, India and the Soviet Union all made conflicting proposals for a settlement of the conflict in Laos which then threatened to assume dimensions capable of jeopardizing the peace of the world. Yet, in the end, it was the proposal made by Prince Sihanouk which was adopted and it was the Prince who was invited to preside over the opening session of a conference which, if it scarcely solved the Laotian problem, at least eliminated its wider perils.[1]

Nor was this an isolated achievement or one wholly attributable to diplomatic skill in the presentation by a relatively disinterested observer of an acceptable compromise. Another official publication bears witness to the degree of international interest and concern evoked by Prince Sihanouk's efforts to uphold the interests of his own country. 'Recent Diplomatic Exchanges concerning the Proposal for an International Conference on the Neutrality and Territorial Integrity of Cambodia'[2] does not, by any means, tell the full story – there is no reference, for instance, to discussions in the United Nations – but the documents it does contain demonstrate the remarkable deference which governments enjoying resources as superior as their policy was different then accorded to the views of Prince Sihanouk.

[1] 'Documents relating to British Involvement in the Indo-China Conflict 1945–1965', Command 2834 of 1965 (H.M.S.O.).
[2] Command 2678 of 1965 (H.M.S.O.).

It is no ordinary ruler who can, more or less simultaneously, be assured that:

'The Government and people of China highly appreciate the policy of peace and neutrality pursued by the Kingdom of Cambodia under the leadership of His Royal Highness Prince Norodom Sihanouk;'

that

'The Soviet Government unswervingly supports the efforts of the Government of Cambodia . . .'

that

'the United States wholeheartedly supports . . . [Cambodian peace and neutrality]'

and that the British Prime Minister endeavours to conciliate by a compliment on his 'wise guidance' as well as by persistent and partially successful efforts to persuade third parties to meet Cambodian wishes.

And what, after all, was all this about? Some incursions, annoying admittedly, but, by comparison with what was going on in Laos and Vietnam, fundamentally insignificant, had been made into Cambodian territory, whereupon Prince Sihanouk had demanded an international conference and, when his demand was finally conceded by those who had initially opposed it, had changed his mind. Whatever view may be taken of the merits of the complex issues involved, one can only admire the dexterity with which this remarkable man exploited conflicting interests to preserve his people and to extract even from those governments whom he had most persistently snubbed a deference as fulsome as it must often have been reluctant.

The success of Prince Sihanouk's juggling of the giants is even more striking when contrasted with Nehru's earlier failure to obtain even the verbal backing of governments hitherto supposed to be particularly amenable to Indian influence. This was in October 1962, when Nehru sent a circular message to the governments of the world asking for their sympathy and support after the Chinese invasion of India. Egypt, Ghana, Iraq, Liberia, Syria, Tanganyika and Yugoslavia, for instance, could scarcely have had much to lose by compliance; all of them had previously been associated with India in joint diplomatic manœuvres by groups of Afro-Asian or 'non-aligned' countries; several had earlier enjoyed Indian diplomatic support at crucial moments; yet all adopted an attitude of neutrality, which Nkrumah carried so far as to declare himself 'distressed and saddened' by the British Government's action in supplying India with military equipment.[1] In 1964 and 1965 the British Government went to considerable lengths to appease Prince Sihanouk, even though his complaints were directed almost exclusively against their American and Thai allies as well as against the South Vietnamese Government then enjoying British sympathy and support. In 1962, however, no government not already hostile towards China or Communism seems to have been willing even to express the view that India had been the victim of aggression.

This is one of the many incidents of recent years which illuminate the limitations of this kind of influence. When nothing of consequence is at stake, or when the

[1] For an interesting analysis of the ups and downs of Indian influence, see: G. H. Jansen, *Afro Asia & Non-Alignment* (Faber & Faber 1966).

conflicting interests of others lend themselves to expert manipulation, a magnetic personality in full control of his own country may hope to sway the votes of foreign governments or, by his own speeches, to evoke sympathetic echoes in others. But, when the chips are down, when India is invaded by China, when Yugoslavia is threatened by Russia, when Egypt is defeated by Israel, the warmest admirers of Nehru, Tito or Nasser are sometimes strangely silent. Personal esteem may not survive the blighting shade of danger or failure. And, when Nkrumah and Sukarno actually fell from power, their personal influence was entirely extinguished; few of their most assiduous sycophants abroad could even summon the courage, or the grace, to murmur a word of regret.

To anyone experienced in the ways of men the fallibility of personal influence should scarcely be surprising, even if it evidently embittered so hardened a politician as Churchill:

> 'Thus then, on the night of the tenth of May, at the outset of this mighty battle, I acquired the chief power in the State, which henceforth I wielded in ever-growing measure for five years and three months of world war, at the end of which time, all our enemies having surrendered unconditionally or being about to do so, I was immediately dismissed by the British electorate from all further conduct of their affairs.'[1]

What is less generally accepted is the equal fallibility, as a reliable source of influence on the actions of foreign governments, of ethical or political principles. It would be unreasonable to reproach the Chinese Government with violating, by their invasion of Indian territory, their

[1] W. S. Churchill, *The Gathering Storm*, op. cit.

undertaking at Bandung in 1955 to refrain 'from acts or threats or aggression or the use of force against the territorial integrity or political independence of any country' or to settle 'all international disputes by peaceful means.'[1] All governments, when their own interests are directly involved, permit themselves considerable latitude in the interpretation of such undertakings, as did the Indian Government when seizing Goa in 1961. What is much more striking is the discrepancy between the utterances, whether at Bandung in 1955 or at Belgrade in 1961, of the representatives of non-aligned, peace-loving governments and the attitudes adopted in 1962 even by those with no immediate cause to fear China or the loss of her favours. It is interesting, for instance, to find the Indian Jansen, in his disillusioned analysis of these events, employing a phrase – 'the double standard' – more often heard on the lips of British Conservatives. But his conclusion is plausible:

'national interests and traditional attitudes were more important than Afro-Asian brotherliness or non-aligned solidarity or moral principles . . . Russia was lukewarm on this issue, and China was Russia's ally, and countries did not want to offend Russia – important to them as a source of economic aid, military assistance or political counter-weight to the West.'[2]

Even Prince Sihanouk often had occasion to complain that the effectiveness of foreign support for his single, and more modest, principle – 'que le Cambodge a le droit d'être laissé en paix et de poursuivre sans être

[1] Declaration of the 1955 Bandung Conference on 'The Promotion of World Peace and Co-operation'.
[2] G. H. Jansen, op. cit.

troublé le destin qu'il s'est choisi'[1] – tended to vary with the circumstances of its enunciation and the particular interests of those concerned. Moreover, when one considers the more ambitious ideas of Nehru, Nkrumah and Sukarno, it is arguable that, far from consolidating their influence, these ideas, to the extent that their authors actually came to believe in them, were responsible for their downfall. If Nehru had not convinced himself that China had been converted to peaceful co-existence and that India's security could rest on this doctrine alone, if Nkrumah had not believed himself the architect of African unity, if Sukarno had not aspired to the leadership of the 'new emerging forces', they, or their successors, might still retain an influence erected on quite other foundations.

If one excludes Nehru, whose leadership of four hundred million people, when allied to his personal qualities, could scarcely fail to invest him with some influence, it is arguable that the other five owed this primarily to their initial domestic success, to a shrewd exploitation of international rivalries and to the inherent, if fortuitous, advantages of their national position. Prince Sihanouk established his ascendancy as the only leader in Indo-China to command the almost undivided allegiance of his people; he played off one outside power against another and he drew strength from his very weakness: Cambodia was defenceless, but none of the Great Powers wished to see it become the seat of another conflict which, on the precedents of Laos and Vietnam, was likely to cost each more than any probable gain. These were opportunities admirably exploited, but even

[1] Command 2678 of 1965.

178

the Prince's most fervent admirers would scarcely accept Lord Hailsham's view that the weakness of his country was a source of spiritual strength or invested him with 'commanding moral authority'.

Nkrumah had an easier hand but overplayed it. As the dynamic leader of a small but relatively prosperous state he could appeal, with his ideas of African unity and opposition to neo-colonialism, to the inhabitants of other African countries less impressed by their own leaders and little conscious of any sense of national identity. As one of the spokesmen of Afro-Asian hostility to the Western Powers he could count on Communist support. But his early successes — the red carpets in Moscow, the deference in international gatherings, the resounding intervention in the Congo — went to his head. He forgot that these were tributes to the degree — unusual for an African leader — of his domestic ascendancy. He thought he had inspired others with an equal faith in his own ideas and he expected his people to meet the cost of his impatience in their propagation. When he fell from power it was as the victim of his own illusions, not the least of which had concerned the practical significance of his international influence.[1]

Sukarno, on the other hand, long manifested a diplomatic skill as striking as the dominance he established over his own countrymen. The Japanese launched him; Australia, India, the Communist countries and the United States backed him against the Dutch; the Americans and Russians were only two of those who

[1] When Nkrumah was deposed, he was visiting China before going on to Hanoi to solve the problem of Vietnam. In this ambition he was not alone, but no other interloper had to pay so dearly for his presumption.

thereafter competed for the favours he avoided bestow-
ing; and, last and least, he became one of the leaders of
the Afro-Asian and non-aligned nations. As long as he
retained Indonesian loyalty and the ability to manœuvre
among the conflicting interests of the Powers, his
influence was assured: no one could dispute the reality
of his local strength and only the British found the price
of his illusory friendship excessive. But he too sur-
rendered to the intoxication of his own ideas and, in the
furtherance of his external ambitions, over-taxed the
patience of his neglected people.

President Nasser may yet encounter a similar fate,
but his undoubted influence has so far been buttressed
by an asset not enjoyed by any of his rivals: the existence
of numerous Moslem and Arabic-speaking peoples
accustomed to look to Egypt for inspiration and finding
no leader of comparable eloquence or personal mag-
netism among their own rulers. He has exploited this
advantage with consistent skill, but it remains to be seen
whether his oratory, his Russian backing, the memory
of his early success over Britain and France and his
diplomatic ability will prevail over the handicaps he has
since imposed on himself: military defeat, the enmity of
so many Arab rivals, commitment to a single Great
Power (one of the major errors of Sukarno's latter
years) and the impoverishment of his own people. In
any case his international influence has passed its
peak and, even in the Arab world to which it is now
largely confined, seems destined to dwindle further.
He too attempted more than his power-base would
support.

Only President Tito continues, with undiminished

dexterity, his virtuoso performance on the international tight-rope. Its foundation was the martial valour of his people in their struggle against the Germans, but the wider influence of Yugoslavia dates from Tito's successful defiance (his Suez) of Stalin in 1948. Tito's heresy immediately made his survival of some interest to all opponents of Communism, while the true believers were equally anxious to prevent his outright apostasy. He has successfully manœuvred between the two camps ever since, yet without dissipating or jeopardizing the true source of his strength: the loyalty of his own people. His advocacy of non-alignment (a concept he has interpreted according to the circumstances of the moment) and his cultivation of the Afro-Asian countries have brought him many minor advantages, but he has never unduly presumed on these or allowed them to interfere with his major interests. Of all our examples his best illustrates the dictum that the most reliable foundation for international influence – other than the intelligent use of power – is a reputation for success.

This is by no means a negligible motive for acceding to the request of a foreign government. We have, after all, excluded from this particular assessment the ability to punish or reward, which is an attribute of the different type of influence based on power. We have recognized that the kind of influence under consideration here is most frequently exerted on questions of no great practical significance to the responding governments and we have selected, as its most objective test, the criterion of votes in the United Nations. Let us then consider the Japanese vote on the issue of Gibraltar. The Japanese Government can have had little reason for hope or fear;

there were no obvious sentimental attachments, preconceptions, interests or precedents to sway them one
way or the other; their reputation for deciding issues on
their ethical merits is not pronounced. What motive
remained? Could it have been the natural desire to find
themselves on the winning side? Does this constitute an
argument of general applicability to the choices of
otherwise undecided governments?

Any authoritative answer to this question would demand a detailed analysis beyond the scope of a brief
essay, but the theory of the 'band-waggon' is widely
accepted in domestic politics and its applicability to
international affairs is at least plausible. On this analogy,
therefore, a national leader first exhibits success by
establishing ascendancy over his own people. He then
impresses his personality on his peers abroad, preferably
accompanying this by a spectacular triumph over foreign
governments – Tito's defection, Suez, New Guinea.
He then seizes on a slogan – non-alignment, anti-
colonialism, peaceful co-existence, Arab nationalism –
calculated to appeal, if not to foreign governments, then
at least to their peoples. The slogan – and his own
personal ascendancy – are then exploited to create a
nucleus of co-operating governments whose representatives vote together in the United Nations and express
similar opinions on international issues whenever this
involves no conflict with the particular interests of each.
If the group can maintain its solidarity – a difficult task
whenever there are several rulers competing for its
leadership – its support becomes sufficiently important
to third countries to attract their adhesion – at least on
matters of relative indifference – in the hope of future

reciprocity. There thus comes into existence an Arab bloc or an Afro-Asian bloc or a non-aligned bloc, which enjoys influence and, in so far as this bloc can be manipulated by one or more member governments, confers this influence on them.

In a simplified analysis this influence is due to the belief of other governments that the backing of President So-and-so will bring a dozen votes in the General Assembly, as many approving speeches and, perhaps, the acquiescence of other governments who may one day want those dozen votes themselves. Every time this belief is confirmed in practice, this success reinforces the expectation of the next and, if neither interest nor overwhelming sentiment dictate otherwise, encourages indifferent governments to support or, at the very least, to avoid opposing, so influential a leader. Even the United States Government went to astonishing lengths — and not only in their words and votes — to conciliate President Sukarno during 1963 and 1964. But this kind of influence not only feeds on its own growth: it depends on growth. Any setback, any intermittence in the record of success, brings an immediate penalty.

This is a phenomenon less characteristic of other kinds of influence. In 1961, for instance, the abortive landing at the Bay of Pigs exposed the United States Government to the judgement of the General Assembly in circumstances conspicuously less favourable and, on most views, less easily justifiable, than those of Britain during the Gibraltar debates of 1967 and 1968. The support accorded to the United States on that occasion was animated by attachment to neither principles nor persons, yet it greatly exceeded anything subsequently mustered by the British Government: 59 governments, with only 13 opposing and 24 abstaining, voted a face-saving resolution urging the docile Organization of American States to take 'such peaceful action as is open to them to resolve existing tensions'. Even in the inter-mittence of power its influence had prevailed, whereas the entirely successful use of definitive force[1] by the Indian Government in seizing Goa – in the same year – was only saved from the censure of the Security Council by the Soviet veto.

If, therefore, we are to seek, on the basis of this admittedly sketchy analysis, a source of influence inde-pendent either of power or of the historical accidents of racial, religious or linguistic affinity, we are driven to conclusions unwelcome to most contemporary British politicians. In the first place all such influence is of less practical significance than other varieties. Secondly it is volatile and undependable. Thirdly, it bears no relation to the virtues or consistency of those who enjoy it. Finally, it is most easily acquired by strong personalities with complete mastery of their own people and able, by their diplomatic dexterity, to display a record of con-sistent, if superficial, success in their international undertakings. Moreover, even if we add to those already mentioned the more illustrious name of de Gaulle, we have to admit that three of the seven have entirely lost the influence thus acquired, that another two are losing it, that Prince Sihanouk's position is precarious[2] and

[1] For a definition of this term and for further analysis of the nature and uses of power see Grant Hugo, op. cit.

[2] On 18 March 1970 he too had to suffer for his addiction to foreign travel, being deposed while on circuit from Paris via Moscow to Peking. His people are likely to suffer still more.

President Tito's more securely based on the esteem of his own people than on his international reputation. Perhaps, after all, even in the long run, power might prove a surer and less inconvenient method, particularly if it could be combined with some of the diplomatic dexterity that need not remain the monopoly of the charismatic and authoritarian.

Influence, no less than prestige, is in the last resort a technique, an instrument for the resolution of disputes. In each case the importance of the concept is inseparable from its efficacity, which depends on its ability to contribute to the achievement of an advantageous terminal situation. Prestige once possessed this capacity, but its now faded mantle has not yet been reliably inherited by influence. And reliability, of which these two abstractions were earlier described as contrasting facets, is a concept that may equally be turned against its own offspring. If influence, however sedulously cultivated by the sacrifice of immediate advantage, can not be relied upon in the hour of crisis, it offers a dubious alternative to the terminal situations indicated by prediction.

These are not, of course, the only abstractions in whose name politicians urge the subordination of the present to the future. Prestige and influence were not selected as typical of such notions, still less of those now most in fashion. Their analysis had two attractions: each was a relatively neutral concept, one which could be employed by governments of very different preconceptions, and each had some obvious practical achievements to its credit. In one sense, therefore, in the sense preferred in these pages, they offered the case for the precedence of long-term considerations at its strongest. Anyone could employ them and some had actually done so successfully.

But the argument against all the other long-term considerations for which no space has been found in the present work does not rest on mere analogy, on the proposition that the weaknesses of the tried and objective must necessarily apply in greater degree to the untested and one-sided. There is a further argument. Whenever immediate gains are sacrificed to ultimate advantage, the assumption must be that, when the ultimate moment arrives, the circumstances will be such that advantage is probable. In other words, the future, in which the deferred harvest is to be reaped, must not be too different from the present. In some historical eras this has been a reasonable assumption. In 1847, when Lord Palmerston laid down the principles of British policy towards China, he could legitimately expect that the environment, the combination of circumstances affecting policy, would be substantially the same twenty years later. In undertaking immediate exertions he could, without undue optimism, count on a later return. Indeed, if he had subsequently been able to analyse the factors affecting Anglo-Chinese relations, not merely in 1867, but in 1887 or even in 1907, it is doubtful whether he would have had much occasion to revise his initial assumptions. For British statesmen, at least, this was an epoch in which the future seemed sufficiently predictable to warrant immediate sacrifices: there was a pattern of evolution which could be made the basis for principles of lasting validity.

This would have been a rash assumption in either 1547 or 1647 and it is still more unsafe today. If we look back to 1947 — a year in which the British Government were still making immense investments, in terms of international relations, in the future — of how many dividends can we now record the payment? If we look forward to 1990, who would venture to predict the state of the world at that time? This is by no means the first period of instability in human history — British politicians, perhaps more than any others, are unduly hypnotized by the altogether exceptional circumstances of the Victorian era — but it is arguable that the pace and extent of change are greater than ever before. Even if we restrict our comparison to the evolution of ideas, Marxism was originated less than a century and a half ago, but its transformation has proceeded ten times more rapidly than that of Christianity: Tito, for instance, nailed his theses to the door about a hundred years later; a millennium and a half elapsed before the appearance of Luther.

Today men no longer plant oaks to provide their grandchildren with shade. The tempests of our times have obscured the horizon and diminished its distance. If we can predict, and plan for, an immediately advantageous terminal situation, we have already achieved much. We have assured our own survival and preserved the options of our children. To sacrifice this certain gain to the abstractions of a hypothetical future is more than an act of faith: it is to desert the solid ground of Reality in pursuit of the will o' the wisp that flits over the swamps of Appearance.

7

END OF ARGUMENT

'Je suis un homme pour qui le monde visible existe.'
Gautier[1]

A S so often happens, the pursuit of abstractions has
carried us far from our purpose: the search for some
alternative to the uncertainties of predicting terminal
situations. To some readers, however, the remoteness of
these variations from the original theme may have been
less distasteful than their monotonous restriction to the
key of method and technique. There has been a persistent assumption that nation-states exist, that they possess
identifiable and conflicting interests, that these conflicts
give rise to disputes and that discrimination between
their Real and their Apparent nature can contribute to
the establishment of a closer relationship between their
intended and their actual consequences. However widely
speculation may have ranged, its purpose has always
been narrow: to assist the decision whether and, if so,
how, to manifest objection to actions defined, with
deliberate tautology, merely as objectionable.

In itself this restriction of the range of inquiry is
defensible. Nobody condemns the surgeon who devotes
a ponderous volume to the diseases of a single section of
the alimentary canal. He is not reproached for ignoring

---

[1] Theophile Gautier. See *Journal des Goncourt* (Charpentier Edition
1888), Vol. I, pp. 181–2.

the processes of swallowing and of elimination. It is not accounted a fault that he neglects the motives with which human beings ingest their nourishment or that he fails to consider the changes that might result from a radically altered diet. He is simply concerned with what actually happens in the pylorus: other aspects of the human condition are for other men to consider.

The surgeon's task, however, is simpler and more innocent than that of the writer on international affairs. Human anatomy does not appear to have undergone any fundamental change for many thousands of years, nor is it often suggested that doctors are required to do more than preserve, to the best of their ability, the functioning of processes that already exist. The human digestive system is manifestly imperfect, but its replacement by something altogether different is not yet envisaged by even the most enthusiastic of medical students and no odium attaches to those who endeavour to patch up and preserve the *status quo*.

This is an odium inescapable by the humblest writer on political technique. Strive as he will for objectivity and neutrality, he can not avoid the commitments and the overtones of the words he uses. The pylorus is not in itself a controversial concept; the nation-state is. Carcinoma presents formidable difficulties in diagnosis and treatment; its nature and its causes are uncertain. Nobody, however, has yet maintained that carcinoma could be beneficial: it is accepted as something to be prevented, if that were possible, and to be cured, if that could be done.

No such consensus of opinion exists concerning the processes of politics, where controversy necessarily attends even the most studiously neutral presentation. The approach adopted in the present work has been to examine a particular aspect of international relations in isolation: to trace the progress of disputes from the commission of an objectionable act to the achievement of a terminal situation. Digressions from this narrow field have been undertaken primarily to demonstrate the distorting influence of wider considerations on the progress of disputes towards their resolution. This is an approach which necessarily begs some rather fundamental questions. For instance, the handling of the Cuban missile crisis was praised for its achievement of a terminal situation that conferred some advantage on both sides and averted the risk of consequences potentially disastrous not only to the parties but to others as well. This is not, however, a verdict universally accepted, least of all by those who might have hoped to escape the adverse effects of thermo-nuclear war between the United States and the Soviet Union. If the unsympathetic comments of the Chinese Government, for instance, were prompted by a comparison of likely terminal situations, this need not only have been because the possibility that the two Super-Powers might end by destroying one another seemed much less appalling in Peking than it evidently did both in Moscow and in Washington. Even in the two latter capitals there might be found a minority ready to proclaim that it was better to risk the destruction of their own nation-state and the death of many millions of their countrymen, than to forego other advantages. These are assumptions alien to the author, but perhaps not to all of his readers.

Even a treatise on method and technique is controversial when it takes for granted that the parties to a dispute each wish to limit its cost to themselves and can — provided these alternatives are clearly envisaged — be expected to prefer an unfavourable terminal situation to one that is finally disastrous. In spite of the obvious historical exceptions this is a possible view. There is a tendency for governments to prefer those solutions which are compatible with the continued exercise of their authority over their own nation-state and, consequently, with the preservation of that nation-state. But, if the arguments in the present work have been directed to the identification of this kind of solution, this expresses the author's preference rather than any general agreement on the desirability of such solutions.

Different approaches are possible. One now fashionable in certain quarters assumes that various aspects of the existing state of affairs in the world are so undesirable that their destruction should take precedence over any other consideration whatsoever. To this school of thought terminal situations and the protracted arguments of this book are irrelevant. What matters is the initial situation, which is regarded as so bad that anything following its destruction must necessarily be better. This is an argument with great attractions for many people. Most human beings are obstinately disinclined to believe that the worst could actually happen. Moreover, even when they admit the possibility of adverse consequences, they argue that these are only potential and consequently uncertain, whereas no doubt is possible concerning the reality of the evil that already exists. To destroy what is certainly bad, they contend, it is worth risking what is only hypothetically worse. Nor are they greatly impressed by the retort that the extent of an evil may be more certain than the possibility of its destruction. A slave, for instance, might be willing to risk extreme perils, even to sacrifice his own life, in order to kill a cruel master. But, if he had any regard for terminal situations, he would not make the attempt unless he had a reasonable expectation that, whatever the cost to himself, he would actually achieve his objective. A mere gesture, the manifestation of an obviously futile intention, would not provide a sufficient incentive to action. On the other hand, the keener his sense of the evil of his present situation, the more he might be inclined to exaggerate the chances of success and to despise the risks and the consequences of failure.

The evident attractions of such reasoning — even to those with much less cause for desperation — are daily demonstrated by reports from all over the world of men killing one another without any very obvious or immediate prospect of thereby achieving a more advantageous terminal situation. Two decades of conflict in Vietnam, the vast unreason of Cultural Revolution among the world's most numerous people, the guerrilla movements spreading across the blotting-paper of the Middle East, the turmoil and the challenge within the United States, the fermenting discontent throughout our fragmented world: these portents of change and dissolution are surely an incongruous background to an essentially conventional theory aimed at the resolution, within an established system of nation-states, of disputes between supposedly rational and sovereign governments.

They are indeed and some optimism is required of anyone who, having no cure to offer for most of humanity's admitted ills, concentrates instead on proposing some trifling ameliorations in the conduct of one small sector of human transactions. Yet this is a sector in which rational notions have already contributed something to the survival of the species. The chance that they might still have more to offer thus provides some compensation for the risk that, in so far as these suggestions are capable of prolonging human lives, they might also be employed to preserve human institutions. Change and adaptation are admittedly as essential to human survival as the avoidance of megadeaths, but extremes of violence and the sudden, rapid and extensive changes earlier described as inherently dangerous have often checked or inhibited the progress that emerges from a series of compromises.

These are antitheses too fundamental to be resolved in a brief exordium. This is a treatise, not of principles, but of methods and techniques. If it takes for granted the heave and thrust of competing nation-states, it is because this process now divides the world. Unless it also destroys the world, it is likely to continue longer than the currency of the present work. Therefore it is worth considering how this turbulence might, to however trivial an extent, be moderated and rationally controlled.

Reason, however, may be invoked in many causes and the constant recurrence, throughout this work, of the refrain of rationality demands some explanation. A course of action that achieves the terminal situation originally intended is rational, as that term has been here employed, but how is the first intention to be judged? What differentiates the desire for a mutually acceptable compromise from the urge for universal destruction? Why should digestion be promoted and the growth of tumours checked?

These are questions which never occur to the surgeon, but which the writer on international affairs can not afford to shirk. His scope may be as limited as his competence, but he must declare himself or forfeit even the barest acceptance by that substantial proportion of readers to whom means are valid only in so far as they translate good intentions to a satisfactory conclusion. Even those able to regard the beginning of a dispute as 'given', may legitimately demand some criterion for judging the ends to which its conduct is directed.

These ends, then, are uncertain, provisional and transitory. They are a misty horizon ever receding before the tentative and erratic advance of the human race. There is only the roughest and vaguest of touchstones to distinguish the oasis from the mirage. But it exists. It is the watershed that divides, however broadly and uncertainly, the urge to enjoy life from the readiness to welcome death, the disciples of Eros from those of Thanatos.

So rhetorical an abstraction is best supported by a historical instance. On 28 July 1914 Gavrilo Princip succeeded, with his revolver, where Čabrinović had failed with his bomb, in killing the Archduke Franz Ferdinand von Österreich Este and his wife, Sophie Duchess of Hohenberg. The motives of the assassins have been examined in great detail, and with conspicuous sympathy, by Vladimir Dedijer in *The Road to Sarajevo*.[1] His verdict on the consequences is more concise: 'the greatest carnage in world history up to that time, devastating much of Europe and causing the

[1] Simon & Schuster, New York 1966.

death of more than ten million people.' This included nearly 16 per cent of those South Slavs for whose sake this murder was ostensibly committed. No concrete advantages are mentioned.

Against these Real consequences Dedijer's closing tribute to the Apparent virtues of Gavrilo Princip and his friends – their 'patriotism, courage and selflessness' – has the hollow clang of the passing bell. His earlier comments are more germane to our central distinction:

> 'Chastity was a strict rule among the Young Bosnians. Zerajić, although a man of twenty-five, never had sexual intercourse, as the Sarajevo police established after his death. Princip confessed the same to Dr. Pappenheim. They did not drink.'

They were described as 'living ascetics for whom physiological life had no meaning.'[1] Princip himself wrote to his purely platonic female friend, Vukosava Čabrinović:

> 'I go from nothingness to nothingness, from day to day, and in me there is less and less of myself.'

It is scarcely possible to imagine a more complete, or a more disastrous, incarnation of the Death Wish, but its final identification as the antithesis of everything argued in the present work emerges most clearly from Princip's later statement to his interrogators:

> 'My thought was therefore only on the success of the assassination; of some unfavourable consequence or other I had not thought at all.'

In those words there peals the Wagnerian trumpet note of the Apparent.

[1] Dedijer, op. cit.

This was not the final manifestation of Thanatos, whose later triumphs were even bloodier, but it was perhaps the most satisfyingly symbolic. It is to the impairment of his future influence, still potent among the embittered old and the idealistic young, that the present work is feebly offered. Its arguments may be as strained as they are imperfect, but its philosophical basis is the simplest of truisms: while there is life, there is hope.

A SELECTIVE BIBLIOGRAPHY

To list all the books to which the author is indebted would over-tax the patience both of his readers and of his publishers, but these are some of those most vividly recalled while writing, together with those quoted in the text or specifically consulted.

FUNDAMENTAL

FREUD, Sigmund – *The Ego and the Id* (tr. James Strachey) 1947, Hogarth, London and Norton, New York 1961; *An Outline of Psycho-Analysis*, Hogarth Press, London and Norton, New York 1949.
VOLTAIRE – *Candide ou l'Optimisme*, numerous editions since 1759.

THEORY OF INTERNATIONAL RELATIONS

ARON, Raymond – *Peace and War: A Theory of International Relations*, Weidenfeld & Nicolson, London and Doubleday, New York 1966.
CARR, Edward Hallett – *The Twenty Years Crisis*, Macmillan, London and New York 1940; *Conditions of Peace*, Macmillan, London and New York 1942.
FARRELL & SMITH (editors) – *Image and Reality in International Relations*, Columbia University Press, New York 1967; *Theory and Reality in International Relations*, Columbia University Press, New York 1967.
HUGO, Grant – *Britain in Tomorrow's World*, Chatto & Windus, London and Columbia University Press, New York 1969.

McNAMARA, Robert S. – *The Essence of Security*, Hodder & Stoughton, London and Harper & Row, New York 1968.

HISTORICAL

ABEL, Elie – *The Missiles of October*, MacGibbon & Kee, London and Lippincott, Philadelphia, 1966.

BULLOCK, Alan – *Hitler* 1952, Odhams Press, London and Harper & Row, New York 1964.

CARR, Edward Hallett – *What is History?* 1961, Macmillan, London and Knopf, New York 1962.

CHAPMAN, Guy – *Vain Glory* 1937, Cassell, London and Dufour, Philadelphia 1968.

CIPOLLA, Carlo M. – *Guns and Sails in the Early Phase of European Expansion* 1965, Pantheon, New York and Collins, London 1966.

CHURCHILL, Winston S. – *The Gathering Storm*, Cassell, London and Houghton Mifflin, Boston 1948; *Their Finest Hour* 1944, Cassell, London and Houghton Mifflin, Boston 1949.

CROSS, Colin – *The Fall of the British Empire* 1968, Hodder & Stoughton, London and Coward-McCann, New York 1969.

DEDIJER, Vladimir – *The Road to Sarajevo*, Simon & Schuster, New York and MacGibbon & Kee, London 1966.

EDEN, Anthony – *Full Circle*, Cassell, London and Houghton Mifflin, Boston 1960.

FEILING, Keith – *Life of Neville Chamberlain*, Macmillan, London 1946

GOULDEN, Joseph C. – *Truth is The First Casualty*, Rand McNally & Co., Chicago 1969.

GRENVILLE, J. A. S. – *Lord Salisbury and Foreign Policy*, Athlone Press, London and Oxford University Press, New York 1964.

GREY, of Fallodon, Lord – *Twenty Five Years*, Hodder & Stoughton, London and Frederick A. Stokes, New York 1925.

HEWLETT, Sir W. – *Forty Years in China*, Macmillan, London 1943.

JAKOBSON, Max – *The Diplomacy of the Winter War*, Harvard University Press Cambridge, Massachusetts, 1961.

JANSEN, G. H. – *Afro-Asia and Non-Alignment*, Faber & Faber, London and Praeger, New York 1966.

A SELECTIVE BIBLIOGRAPHY

KEESING'S CONTEMPORARY ARCHIVES

KENNAN, George F. – *Memoirs* 1967, Little Brown, Massachusetts and Hutchinson, London 1968.

KENNEDY, Robert F. – *13 Days*, Macmillan, London and Norton, New York 1969.

L'ETANG, Hugh – *The Pathology of Leadership*, Heinemann Medical Books, London 1969.

MANCHESTER, William – *Death of a President*, Harper & Row, New York and Michael Joseph, London 1967.

MORRIS, James – *Pax Britannica*, Faber & Faber, London and Harcourt Brace and World, New York 1968.

MORSE & MACNAIR – *Far Eastern International Relations*, Houghton Mifflin, Boston 1931.

NICOLSON, Harold – *Lord Carnock*, Constable, London and Houghton Mifflin, Boston 1930; *Peacemaking* 1919, Constable, London and Houghton Mifflin, Boston 1944; *Curzon: The Last Phase*, Constable, London and Houghton Mifflin, Boston 1937.

PANIKKAR, K. M. – *Asia and Western Dominance*, Allen & Unwin, London and John Day, New York 1953.

STRANG, Lord – *Britain in World Affairs*, Faber & Faber, London and Praeger, New York 1961.

SCHLESINGER, Arthur M. – *A Thousand Days*, Andre Deutsch, London and Houghton Mifflin, Boston 1965.

TAYLOR, A. J. P. – *The Origins of the Second World War*, Hamish Hamilton, London and Atheneum, New York 1961; *The Struggle for Mastery in Europe 1848–1918*, Oxford University Press, London and Harcourt Brace and World, New York 1957.

THOMAS, Hugh – *The Suez Affair*, Weidenfeld & Nicolson, London and Harper & Row, New York 1966.

THORNE, Christopher – *The Approach of War 1938–9*, Macmillan, London and St. Martins, New York 1967.

WOODRUFF, Philip – *The Men Who Ruled India* 1954, Jonathan Cape, London and Schocken Books, New York, 1964.

STRATEGIC THEORY

BUCHAN, Alastair – *War in Modern Society*, C. A. Watts, London and International Publishing Service, New York 1966.

HORELICK, Arnold L. & RUSH, Myron – *Strategic Power and Soviet Foreign Policy*, University of Chicago Press, 1966.

KAHN, Hermann – *On Escalation*, Praeger, New York and Pall Mall Press, London 1965.

WOLFE, Thomas W. – *Soviet Strategy at the Crossroads*, Harvard University Press, New York and Oxford University Press, London 1964.

OFFICIAL PUBLICATIONS

British Documents on the Origins of the War – ed. Gooch & Temperley, H.M.S.O.

Documents Concerning German-Polish Relations and the Outbreak of Hostilities between Great Britain and Germany on September 3 1939 – Command 6106 – H.M.S.O. 1939.

Documents Relating to British Involvement in the Indo-China Conflict – Command 2834 – H.M.S.O. 1965.

On Events in Czechoslovakia – Press Group of Soviet Journalists – Moscow 1968.

Recent Exchanges Concerning Attempts to Promote a Negotiated Settlement of the Conflict in Vietnam – Command 2756 – H.M.S.O. 1965.

Recent Diplomatic Exchanges Concerning the Proposal for an International Conference on the Neutrality and Territorial Integrity of Cambodia – Command 2678 – H.M.S.O. 1965.

INDEX

The theoretical concepts with which this book is principally concerned are indicated in capital letters — CANT

INDEX

INDEX

INDEX